YouTube Alchemy
The 90 Day Six Figure Revolution

Abe Cano

in Association with
Kindle Direct Publishing

Chapter Index:

Author's Note:

The first hurdle for me was condensing this book down to a crunchable word count to not only save on cost production but ensure it could be purchased at a great price.

I wanted the discouraged, downtrodden and hungry to get this book and read it- before the wolves did. Some of the most influential books I ever read (Think and Get Rich) were pocket sized reads that I gladly paid what most bloated non-fictionals fetch. The word count has never been a buy/hold flag for me, as long as I smell meat on the bone.

I wanted this to be the Cliff Notes version at a bargain, but as I hammered my way through the first quarter I realized how difficult that would be.

You'll need to see the future of video and why it's so special. You'll need to rethink your strategy and get on board with the executives at Google that have your best interests at heart (I promise!)
There is an actual system in this book; a parts list with nuts and bolts and strange looking gizmos that you'll need to assemble. There's a little math involved and you might need to dog-ear a page or two to recheck your specs.

I wanted this to be inspiring and entertaining enough to read from cover to cover, because I knew the "Patent- Pending" part would get thick in some places.

Creating a technical manual for building a content portfolio of click-generating engines would've been gobbled up by tech moguls already in the know- so I had to make it fun.

Long story short, the book was too chunky to be a field guide (Rats!)

I hope if you're reading this you're one of the tired, down-trodden and hungry individuals that are looking for a way to beat the odds- because you've found it. In your hands is the instruction book to building these marvelous click-generating engines that will spit pennies, dimes and quarters into a digital account every day. How many of these machines you build is up to you. Who you choose to run them is up to you. Make wise decisions and don't be greedy, there is plenty of money to go around. With that said, I want to congratulate you for getting this far... Newton would be proud. Tesla is looking down from his time machine cheering; "Don't stop now!!"

We are the tinkerers and inventors. The visionaries that instinctively know in our guts a wellspring must exist that we can lay hold to. We are the entrepreneurs, the come-back kids, the bootstrap millionaires. I tip my hat to you and wish you the best of success.
Abe

Introduction:

It is my hope that readers will not only understand why Youtube is the wave of the future but how it will shift our focus in technology like no other time before.

Youtube's total market capital in 2015 was in the neighborhood of 300 Billion Dollars. They are not trying to punish creators for making their business plan profitable, but instead they are leveling the playing field for innovators to have a fighting chance at this game. The money is real, and the wealth is attainable like no other time in history. My goal in creating this book was not only to inspire you to take charge of your business like Youtube wants you to, but to understand the ethical and professional practices it wishes to see in the future.

Youtube wants to continue building on momentum, not inhibiting it, but to do so must mean regulation and awareness for everyone across the board.

They are also seeing negative trends emerge that are affecting the world (quite literally.)

Open discussion is important, freedom of speech is important- but in many contexts, Youtube does not want to reward bad behavior. They are trying to curtail the capitalization of troll bait and destructive dialogue evolving to generate money.

I can't say that I was asked to write this book for Youtube in response to the massive backlash for it's changes- but I can say that I share the same goals and vision that this organization has for its future. It's critical you understand how powerful the digital era of news media will impact our culture and finance. You will find this book both a strategy guide and a treasure trove of information.

This is a collaboration of hundreds of content creators that will not only demystify Youtube's Monetization policy but show you how Youtube envisions a professional and fair partner relationship. With greed comes reckless abandonment of the core principles that make not only businesses work but our societies coexist in harmony.

With that said, this guide will also inspire and energize you to think differently about money and how it's made. It was created from a "millionaires" perspective to help you see the "big picture."

As a person that learns easiest by example, I use the second chapter of Youtube Alchemy to give you some background on how money works and how to see it with new eyes.

It may surprise some readers that I start with the founding father of Alchemy himself; Sir Isaac Newton, but I promise this book is more than a hypothetical synopsis.

These concepts are as real as trading shares on the NASDAQ. It may sound impossible to the average layman that one could double and triple their money, compounding increases and eventually become a millionaire, but everyday a new handful of tenacious day traders do just that.

Don't be deceived; there is some order in who gets rich and who stays poor, making these methods difficult. Heavy regulation and restrictive limitations have been put in place to limit the broad implications of a wealthy society. The system does not work if there are too many chiefs and not enough Indians.

Newton was not experimenting with Alchemy for greed, but rather as a way to break the metaphorical chain around mankind's neck; specifically the buying and trading power of gold. It was for this reason and despite his remarkable achievements in science and mathematics, that the Demagogues spun Newton as nothing more than a heretic and garden variety magician. Centuries later, when the Academics could safely distance themselves from the lash of the almighty scepter, Newton was eventually credited for the genius he was.

Sadly, this means there is a real possibility that the machines discussed in this book could also come under scrutiny. I believe that time is yet a ways off and there will still be many who read this these words that don't apply its principles. It should go without saying though, that publicizing such blueprints means "The Cat is out of the Bag" and how long it stays out remains to be seen.

Furthermore, those that follow the steps to building the engines that power their machines may simply lack the amount of time and energy it takes to maintain them. From the moment you choose to use this strategy you must make a commitment to it in the same way a stock broker does when he sets aside his money for investment. Though the infrastructure of this digital industry requires no grease or fuel or iron, it requires your time and innovation and that is worth money!

To have a successful run with this you must value your time and energy as you would working a 9-5 job. There is a method here, follow it. There are blueprints, use them. There are workers out there- employ them.

The question is not "if you will make any money on Youtube", it is "how much" and "for how long." If your timeframe is limited to a matter of days or even weeks, consider most startup companies often take years to turn a profit. Fear not, this will not take years or even A Year, but you must make the same commitment to it that any good executive makes to a new business.

Mineral Exploration is probably one of the most risky businesses to get into, and yet many investors put their dollars on the line digging for precious metals they often aren't guaranteed to find. Youtube is your mountain of dirt, beneath its surface are crusts of gold just sitting there waiting for you to unearth them. I am giving you the coordinates and machines to excavate with; it's up to you to get your hands dirty and do the work. Eventually you'll start hiring employees to do the heavy lifting and manual labor, working yourself further and further away from the piles of rock and dust. Once you get the hang of it you'll invest in more rigs and replicate the same system and hire supervisors to replace yourself. But you gotta start with a shovel in your hand, and I am giving you a lot more than a shovel.

To my Uncle Ron and Aunt Ann, for inspiring the idea

Chapter 1
How Youtube is Changing Media

If you are new to Youtube and looking to cash in on the most exciting place to build financial freedom, you are getting on the bus at a truly revolutionary time. For those already in the know and who've made their fortunes on this platform, this chapter sheds light on the recent changes that could dramatically affect your revenue earnings.

This book is about building wealth, and doing it quickly with a clean and neat strategy that encompasses a respect for Youtube, the global community and Advertisers. If you can learn by example, and follow this system, your path to riches will be bright and un-hindered.

If you are stuck in the old mentality of how to get viewers on Youtube, this book will clarify how the new Youtube looks at advertiser/channel relationships and where to find new revenue streams.

Let's talk about Youtube:

There's just no way around it, the 'Tube is showing the world it's the super power of video media. Facebook is struggling to find a way to promote its "Live" feature and Twitter is even toying with applications that could eventually include Snap-Chat like implications.

This is not just a horse and buggy show, media is a multi-billion dollar industry and continues to grow at an alarmingly fast rate. As Youtube grows, Hollywood producers and Cable networks are feeling the pinch as Advertisers spend more of their money for online media spots.

Large media corporations have begun turning their sights on Youtube. Where many TV studios are suffering nasty declines in viewers and promoter advertising, Youtube news agencies like Young Turks are continually increasing their annual revenue.

To make it a fair game for all, the suits inside Google's strategic enterprise are moving to regulate the large scale domination of media giants. This is something you as a small fish should be rejoicing over! It means that Youtube intends to completely revolutionize and broaden the playing field for entrepreneurs who have the right business strategy.

What I can guarantee you will learn from this book is not only a new perspective on how to grow your business but how to do it in the most efficient and agreeable way (the "White Hat" SEO way not the troll/manipulator's way.) But we'll dig into that later.

Youtube's cash comes from Advertisers, so understanding the advertising perspective will help you build a better business strategy. Advertisers understand the psychological link between their commercials and the media used to channel it to the consumer.

Right now the grassroots evolution of journalism on Youtube is just starting to capitalize on news. They are reaping the rewards of creating really controversial news stories for the benefit of more viewers. However, the trending dialogue is becoming more slanted towards demonizing the "1%" and "their corporate illuminati" while at the same time profiting heavily from their pockets.

Luxury sedan manufacturers are not going to be so keen on placing their ads on a video titled; "Is it time to hang the bankers?"

In the sense, creators of this anti-capitalist discussion are not only shooting themselves in the foot, but they are being hypocritical from a business perspective.

Youtube is not deleting anyone's channels. You can still create anti-establishment content, but just realize that advertisers (not Youtube) are part of the "establishment" that makes this system work. They are not going to pay for advertising that attacks the foundation their companies are built on, and rightly so.

Now before you start hailing the "end to freedom of speech" or even the "martyrdom of free press" please realize that this has happened before, not only in newsprint but television advertising. It was all happening probably before you were born and outside of your league. The "Madmen era" of advertising had to deal with these very same issues in the 60's, 70's, 80's and 90's. You are a newbie to this so of course it's going to seem confusing.

Advertising agencies spend millions of dollars in research to protect themselves from harmful PR.

Campbell's Soup does not want its commercials playing on a video that calls for Vegan Jihad. A Vegan Jihad might be really controversial and get lots of views but if your video is about food, the advertisements on your video will probably be food-related.

Campbell's Soup does not care if you make Vegan Jihad videos, they just want to sell their chicken soup to people that like eating chicken soup.

If you make that difficult for them, why would they give you money?

You'll find lots of secrets in this book... much of which Youtube has never shared with the public.

Lots of changes are coming; the Adsense Monetization restructuring is just one of many.

On the horizon is Youtube Red, a paid premium service with no advertisements. Though it's in the beta stageYoutube is toying with many ideas, some strikingly similar to Netflix' original series.

Youtube Red will give viewers premium access to new on demand features and create a less volatile environment that is not advertiser backed.

This means there may be a completely new way to earn money by participating in exclusive Youtube Red broadcasting that is not affected by picky advertisers.

With that said, Youtube will probably only extend this program to channels with high integrity and "good credit" (as discussed in later chapters.)

Youtube understands its success belongs to the little guys; the people that are making unique and interesting content to share with the world. There is also a close knit community framework tied to Youtube that no other media company has succeededin replicating.

In the next chapters I go over everything from creating a network of "machines" (a virtual media portfolio) to how Youtube gives a virtual "credit score" to your channels.

I show you how to see your channel management as a business and how Adsense (aka The Bank of Google) is a prestigious financial institution worthy of respect and proper business dealing.

As you will read later, even colleges and Universities will begin offering courses centered around Youtube and Adsense Monetization. Degrees in broadcast journalism and media production will be among the hottest most in- demand jobs in the next five years.

Reading this book is just the tip of the iceberg, but it is the hope of mine and many others that it inspires you to do good work, find new niches and build a profitable business that will last for years to come.

Chapter 2
Thinking Like Newton

Alchemy though widely lauded as esoteric folklore, is not a mythical fabrication. It exists, was patented, streamlined and materialized in the lifetime of the man who Godfathered it; Sir Isaac Newton. Up until the time Newton had been tinkering with the philosophy of Alchemy, currency was a relatively useless mechanism and poorly conceptualized by those that used it (i.e.; the Roman Empire.) Unless the coins were struck in gold, silver or bronze the value of non-precious metal based currency like Shekels were about as frowned upon as accepting Bitcoin in 2013. Newton died in 1726, but he lived to see Alchemy's inception in 1690 when the Massachusetts Bay Colony issued the first paper currency in America. Newton had carried out the bulk of his research as an English Citizen under the English/Scottish Kingdom of King William III and Queen Anne. England strong armed it's currency under the conservative lordship of a gold backed system. A newly colonized America was the most progressive and least regulated country of its time- a safe haven for the innovators that drafted the concepts forging capitalism.

Don't worry the history lesson is almost over.

You need to know that Newton was seeking a "Philosopher's Stone" not a "Chemist's Stone." The Philosopher's Stone is the mythical precept in Alchemy that enabled Alchemists to fabricate gold. The Philosopher's Stone was simply a philosophy that under writ the antiquated worship of the sacred yellow rock at the basis of nearly every ancient civilization. The Romans were aware of the inevitable demise of Gold. It was at the bequest of Greek and Roman bureaucrats that leading Philosophers of the day find an alternative resource to crude "stones." The debate attracted an eccentric crowd of scholars and magicians.

Newton dabbled in chemistry as he did in astronomy, but the output of his tinkering was what gave us modern day Calculus; a mathematical language that led us to decrypt the mysteries of our universe. For the Cambridge genius, cooking up recipes for gold would've been far below his logic and reasoning. He knew, (with good reason) that a philosophy could exist, challenging the Biblical sacredness of Gold. That was the real reason he was called a heretic and ostracized for his research.
He was confident that his ideas would catch wind, and indeed they did- but I will leave you to chase those rabbits. Though the founding fathers of the United States lay dark oaths against a banking system exorcising such sorcery, they could not stop gold from becoming obsolete. Thomas Jefferson forewarned his colleagues of the conspiracy to stray from a non-metallic currency, but his cries went largely unheeded. Even back then, paper currency and a debt based system was a lucratively attractive prospect; a new philosophy built on the magic of creating gold out of thin air.
I don't propose to reinvent the wheel in this book, I just want you to see money the way Isaac Newton saw gold. Money is not real, it's just paper- and even if we stop using money, gold still won't be a sustainable option for meeting supply and demand. Don't believe me? Just ask the Romans.

"The Philosopher's Stone" is better translated in modern times as "The Money Mechanism" a system that uses credit and debt to offer values on physical products. The stock market was created to leverage money by suggesting future value of not only physical objects but even ideas that now form the framework for modern companies like Facebook and Twitter.

But enough about that, understand the world's richest people make their money off this system. The world is changing fast, it is in a slinky effect right now and technology is jumping ahead of printed currency. Cryptocurrency will probably replace paper currency, but it's still a long ways off. Regulators will find a way to corral that system too, and it won't be long before debt and credit is exchanged by using Bitcoin.
Even so, the slinky effect will catch up with cryptocurrency and the banking system will find innovative ways to marginalize and safeguard its capitalization.

Where am I going with all of this?

My next book already in the process of publishing is; "The Big Float"

It talks in greater detail about the fundamentals of money creation, how we make it and where it comes from. In the book, I talk about how money is moved around in chunks; big chunks, medium chunks, small chunks etc. Rich people know how to move bigger chunks of money. They see money differently.

Poor people stay poor because smaller chunks move faster and are easier to chase. Naturally, poor people tend to do whatever solves their financial problems in the quickest fashion, requiring less commitment. It may be rewarding or out of necessity in some cases, but chasing small chunks of money will just keep you in a revolving cycle of debt and poverty.

I want you to read this book like you're already rich.

Understand that the end result of this book is teaching you how to wrap your head around larger chunks of money.

This isn't voodoo; it's just practical business sense that works.

Read and have fun with it.

Let's talk about digital money, because that's what makes the Youtube Machine work.
Money is simply digital numbers.
Online these digital numbers talk to other digital numbers called bits and bytes.
The digital numbers are just cogs turning in gears made of bits and bytes.
The gears made of bits and bytes turn when commands are given to them.
Commands are dispersed by batches of orders called Clicks.
Youtube is a machine that releases set amounts of commands for every batch of clicks it receives.

Clicks are made by viewers, who make split second decisions based on impulses.
These impulses are precious commodities, because humans use impulses to spend their money.
Companies want to capture a percentage of these impulses so humans will buy their products.
As a fair trade for the impulses, Companies put some of their money into the Youtube Machine to get as many impulses as they can.

Some of you will argue that more goes into the advertising and click-ration for viewer impressions, but I would prefer you get away from thinking about viewer impressions altogether.
Think bigger, more expansive and more innovative.
Let the Advertisers do their job and focus on content creation and viewer relationships.
Allowing yourself to be driven by daily SEO stats can really weigh on the intuitive nature of building positive connections with your viewers. I am not saying to throw the baby out with the bath water, but at least for now, while your portfolio is in the 90 day startup period, put aside advertising and focus on view count.

It may seem redundant, but you will be building the engines that run miniature Youtube machines.
The blueprints for these machines are fairly simple and you will need to practice building them until you can duplicate them quickly and efficiently.
Once you have set up a stockpile of these machines, you will service them regularly (on a daily or weekly basis). Each machine is unique, but you service it the same way and in the same fashion as all the other machines. Your collection of machines will be your portfolio; you will manage these machines like businesses, because they bring you little bits of money every day.
Once you have successfully established your service schedule, you can hire employees to service the machines which will free you up to make new machines. Once you are satisfied with how much money these machines are generating on a daily basis, you can hire a supervisor to manage the employees that service your machines.

It's that simple.

Big Fish Little Fish
In the coming chapters, I am assuming you are a little fish. I wrote the book with the average Joe in mind, because I have a heart for helping others succeed. For the big fish reading this book, it is only going to help you leverage more power to get rich faster. All you little fishes listen up; you have tough competition from the sharks that are absorbing every word that I write- but you DO have an advantage. You may be small, but your ideas and creativity will give you a hands on edge that the bigger fish can only hope to hire. Your goal is to make each machine (or business) as innovative as possible. You have time on your side, the ability to research trends and chase exciting news stories. All you have to worry about now is collecting good news stories every day, turning those into content, labeling/tagging them correctly and shooting them off to your machines. Don't sweat it, I will show you exactly how to do everything. Be confident that if you're reading this book you are one of those brilliant, out of the box thinkers that the Big Fish are looking for.

If you are a disorganized person, I highly suggest buying a wall sized white board to keep track of each machine (each Youtube Channel) that you build. Separate these into columns so you can track and date each product (each video) that you disseminate weekly.

As you will see, my goal for you as a small fish is to build a well-oiled machine and once you have mastered and are comfortable with how to operate it, duplicate the system 10 times.
This does not mean creating the same product for each machine. Each channel will be unique, and each product (video) will fall in line with the type of Channel you've created.
If you make a celebrity gossip channel, each video you make for that channel will only be Hollywood gossip related. If you make a food channel, each video you make for that channel will be food related. With this in mind however, your system will be simplified across the board and will follow the same patterns as the other channels.

Each day you will research trending subjects for each of these channels. Once you have identified your hot button topics, you will sequentially lay them out according to their corresponding categories.
I recommend ten channels because it is an even number and the easiest method to calculate the sales generated.

Initially however, you will start with one channel and systematically work your way up in even numbers. You will duplicate the first channel and work with two until you are comfortable with the pace and workload required to operate two. When you have mastered two, duplicate those channels so you have four. Repeat until you are pushing out content to ten channels.
Overwhelmed? Don't be. It sounds like a lot of work, but in the coming chapters we will break every part of this down until you can do it in your sleep. When you have reached ten channels you are no longer a small fish but a medium fish, and you can begin hiring small fish to help you maintain your machines.

Making your first Million
Let's break for a second and talk about the real reason you bought this book. I hope you made this investment with becoming wealthy in mind, because that is exactly what we intend to do. So let me warn you, getting wealthy is a job- a tough one- and you better learn to like it.

I truly wish someone had given me this book when I first left high school, but the internet had barely been invented.
We are now at a ripe time for making more millionaires than any other time in history. It's true that people are getting smarter, but don't get it twisted; this is only half the battle. Generating wealth takes sweat blood and tears, so be prepared to give lots and lots of it!

The good thing is, from scratch these virtual machines do not cost any money to build. They require time but if you are a small fish you have plenty of that!
And no, I'm not talking about years and years of time, I'm referring to quality hours of nose to the grind

stone time. Do whatever is necessary to devote more time to this job, because the quicker you get your machines up and running, the earlier you can switch to doing this full time. And trust me, you'll want to! This is a fun job, and once you get the hang of it, it's actually pretty simple.

Youtube is different than most areas of commerce in the content creation sector.

This is the reason I chose Youtube as the main machine for building my wealth.

I am an excellent blogger, and made my first thousand dollars building blogs and selling them, but the return on investment for that route was too slow.

When I began cultivating blogs to sell to business owners I also felt like I hit a brick wall. I didn't like passing off my hard work to someone else.

There are lots of people that make full time blogging a lucrative business but I promise you; Youtube has made more millionaires than any other media outlet available.

I was and still am a stock trader, so I am accustomed to seeing my ledger increase by closing bell.

For me, Youtube was like trading stocks- the channels are literal money barrels that fill up at the end of every day and every week. I can check my monetization stats and see real dollars and cents adding up across all channels.

Youtube traffic converts to tangible, real-time money and that's why I use this system.

With stocks I am buying my shares at low prices and holding till enough buyers raise the price.

With Youtube I am creating my shares out of thin air, and viewers are the buyers.

Someone else may see it differently, but I knew a good thing when I saw it, and have never looked back.

The large majority of people trying to make Youtube work fail. I come across dormant channels all the time that have videos with a few thousand views. For most people it never occurs to them that a few thousand views is actually a pretty decent success.

This is where a replicated system comes into play; when you are managing ten channels that have 5,000 views on each video, that's a combined 50,000 views across the board.

Most people become discouraged that they'll never reach a million views or a million subscribers, yet that goal becomes much more attainable when spread out ten times.

Getting 100,000 views is not impossible. Getting 50,000 views is even easier.

This system does not catapult you into six figures overnight, but neither does trading stocks -if you're just starting out.

The difference between making your millions on Wall Street and making your millions on Youtube is that you don't need any money to make videos.

To truly benefit from this book you must start seeing each video and each channel as an investment in your portfolio. Collectively they will grow interest every day and every week.

You will even make money while you're sleeping, because the internet never sleeps.

I have had hundreds of videos go viral overnight (OK so for me going viral is a lot different.)

If I have a video I forgot about from two weeks ago hit 50,000 views before I've ate breakfast, I consider that a win.

This is something I go into later on, because you will always have big winners that make up for slow movers. It's a balance. Again, it's like the stock market, some of my stocks outperform others by long shots. On the days that I have big spikes I rarely notice the runts. With Youtube I never have to worry about the value of my shares going down. The videos will always be there and they are always gaining interest.

By now you may be wondering what a reasonable expectation is for making a million dollars on Youtube, and I am not going to weigh in on that.

This book is called Youtube Alchemy, not making millions on Youtube (although if you follow this process it will happen.)

Even if you totally fudge your projects up, a hard working content creator WILL make six figures with this system. The strategy is a 90 day, 120 video method that will compound virtual interest over a set course of time. Your goal should be making six figures in no less than 12 months. That is a really long time for most successful content creators. If you stick to your guns and put in the hours, you can reach the six figure mark in half the time.

Only you can determine how much time you can devote to your businesses.

To get there faster you could hire other fish to help you, and we will discuss that in later chapters.

For now, rest assured the Youtube Machine has already made more millionaires than regulators wish to admit.

Just hang on and enjoy the ride!

Viewers are Customers

The first mistake people make when setting up a Youtube channel is failure to know their audience. The people
that will be watching your videos are like shoppers in your store, without them you can't make any money at all. If you have created a channel without your audience in mind, you might as well start over with a
fresh clean slate.

Am I seriously asking you to delete your channel?
If you haven't designed an audience-oriented business plan YES, I am.
The reason will be explained in full, but before we go into details, I want you to understand how the audience
works for your benefit. It is far more than advertising or traffic and well beyond the mark of getting "X" amount of subscribers.
Viewers are customers, so I want you to start envisioning them as such. Your channel is a store front and it
has products to sell to these customers. Your customers are also proverbial miners- they are scouting the web
every day looking for bits of information to mine and collect into storehouses. You may not see the information

they are looking for as a "product" but indeed, everything they are looking for is essentially either a product

service or solution. Businesses in all faucets of society use this same method of determining how to categorize or "tailor-make" their business plans to suit the needs of their customers in this fashion; product, solution or service. I will typically use the word "product" to save time, but it could also mean solution or service.

Don't get too hung up on what you're offering yet- as long as you realize your channel is a store front and

your viewers are the customers, you are ready for the next step.

A successful business is built on a rock solid business plan- you need one. Don't get frustrated and don't stop

reading simply because this sounds too "outdated" -I assure you, this book is far more than a business plan.

Let's pretend you already have a channel dedicated to doing product reviews. You are a good looking (attractive) person, you have a high definition camera and your set looks professional. You have on average

100-2,000 viewers but the traffic is never consistent. It appears that you are doing everything right, but are

gaining few if any new subscribers - at this point your channel is stagnating.

The scenario above is a typical breaking point for many- but they are tapping out too early... everything you

believe about successful video production is probably incorrect.

That's because a successful channel has nothing to do with your physical attractiveness, professionalism or

even quality of camera. These things may or may not help in the long run, but it certainly doesn't make or

break a successful business owner; YOU.

Let me help you understand why; for businesses that sell in-demand products, they rarely worry about aesthetics

or professionalism. Don't get me wrong, these are not bad things to incorporate into a well-honed business, but

again- they 'alone' don't spell success.

You could be a business professional dressed in the nicest suit selling lemonade at music festival, but if a raggety bum was setup next door selling cold beer it leaves little imagination as to who would make more money.

That's why big corporations like Walmart can get away with having long lines of customers waiting to check out

their purchases. People may grumble about waiting in line but at the end of the day it doesn't stop them from shopping in Walmart's stores. Walmart knows their products are high in demand and they know there is a reasonable expectation for them to deliver these goods.

People are willing to stand in line for good products.

The same is true for you the business owner and the product you are offering to your customers.
It is true that many Youtube stars blindly fell into "luck" and discovered they had a knack for creating some
kind of "product" the audience loved. But they are the exceptions, and you shouldn't base your business plan on
any particular Youtube channel, you will fail!

That may sound too hard to believe, but there are millions of content creators that make their own videos
without EVER getting in front of the camera. They hire people to create the content and do the voiceovers. They
build channels on ideas, and gain millions of subscribers, defying the conventional methods of most popular
Youtubers.

There are literally BILLIONS of niche markets waiting to be developed into Youtube channels. There are
virtually no limits to the "products" you could "sell" to your customers.
The only thing that matters is how In-demand these products are and how many customers out there are willing to
stand in line to get them.

I hope this is making sense to you. If you need to re-read the first few paragraphs of this chapter then do so
now. You cannot run a successful channel without understanding the business/customer relationship of Youtube.

The Great thing about Youtube is that your customer base will come from every part of the world- all you have
to do is find out how many customers exist out there. You do not need to find them- they will come to you.
I'm going to use the example of Pets, and narrow our customer base down to "Dog owners"- let's narrow that down
even further to "Chihuahua Owners".

Chihuahua Owners are "our" customers. Our channel is the store that will focus only on these customers. For
this example, it doesn't matter if the customers are new dog owners, breeders or just enthusiasts- they all
have one thing in common and that's Chihuahuas.

A quick research will show us that there are 20,000 breeders in the U.S. alone and 42,000 in Europe. We know
that there are probably more owners and enthusiasts than breeders, so we could safely estimate there are 62,000
customers for sure, but perhaps twice as many enthusiasts and owners. That'd put the number at 124,000
customers.

That is a LOT of customers! You may be discouraged that you won't get a million customers coming to your
business, but you don't need a million customers. Get away from the myth that you need a million subscribers to
be a millionaire Youtuber! You don't!

You are a multi-business owner and this is just ONE of your many businesses.
Out of these 124,000 customers you could have 20,000 to 30,000 repeat customers- these are people that will
come to your store every day to buy your products. Don't worry about finding the die-hard customers, they spend
their ever waking moments scouting the World Wide Web for a place to buy their products. Youtube knows who they
are, and when they see your new store offering a product that these customers are searching for, Youtube will
suggest your store to them.

Let's go back.

Remember we talked about the business plan? You will need to create a new business plan for every single store
(i.e.; Channel) you open. We know one of our stores will sell products to Chihuahua enthusiasts, so that is
where our first business plan will begin.

In this plan we layout the blueprints for our product; what we will sell and how we will sell it.
We can answer this by returning to the concepts of what a product is; product, solution, service.
Some of our customers will come to us seeking a solution. That may be as simple as "How to train my Chihuahua
puppy to stop chewing"
Some of our customers will come to us seeking a product "Chihuahua T-shirts" or "Rottweiler coffee mugs"
Some of our customers will come to us seeking a service; "Chihuahua stud service" or "Chihuahua obedience

classes."

Even if what you are selling is the news, it still provides a service because people want to stay in touch with what is going on and you are bringing it to them.

I hope you are taking notes, or maybe getting a highlighter and marking this part of the book. These simple
templates apply to any and every product you could offer through your store.
We will talk about these products later on when referring to "Choosing a Processor." I refer to this category
of videos and video channels as "Slow" processors because they do not make the Youtube machine tick quite as
fast (Don't worry we will get into "Fast" processors soon enough.)

This is just the beginning and we have a long way to go before you learn the secret to creating a successful channel. Not only will you be able to build machines that are literal viewer flytraps you will learn how to duplicate them to maximize the money they generate.

Chapter 3
Building The Machines

You know how in college you always had that one favorite teacher that would stomp their foot to alert you that
the subject matter they were covering would be "on the test"?
This is me stomping my foot; "I highly recommend you read this whole chapter! Even if you already have a
Youtube channel and even if you already use Adsense!"
This will make the difference between failing and winning, and I will only play the world's smallest violin for
you when you fail miserably for not reading every part of this chapter!

This is more than just teaching you about technical data, it's "HOW" you see and perceive this technical data
that makes ALL THE DIFFERENCE.
If you do not follow these steps from the beginning, these machines will not work. Plain and simple.

Setting Up A Google Adsense Account

This is my favorite part! The Adsense Account is like your virtual bank account. For my own intent and
purposes you'll see me refer to the Google Adsense Account sometimes as the "The Google Bank," the "Bank of
Google" or in a more familial term "Uncle Sugar."
Opening up an account with the "Bank of Google" is like applying for a loan at the "Bank of Warren Buffet"
It is a digital bank, so you can't see the granite floors, mahogany desks or 600 thread count curtains hanging
from the windows- but trust me, in a physical world they'd be there!
You'd see executives in fine Italian suits conversing with young stock traders wearing Gucci watches and $700
haircuts.
This is THE Rolls Royce of modern finance, and this is where YOU are submitting your application!
So let's say you've got all the necessary paperwork, you're wearing your Sunday best and looking sharp. You're
standing in line, waiting to make your big pitch to the senior loan consultant that "YOU have what it TAKES to
be an integral part of this industry".
 You happen to glance behind you and see a sloppy line of people, wearing nothing but flip flops, bath robes
and some are even blabbing loudly on their phones about how hungover they are. It frightens you to think that

some of these people have the nerve to walk into a place like this and expect to be approved for a loan.
Those people make up 90% of the demographic submitting their applications to Google Adsense!
It is no wonder they fail! They don't see the big picture! They have no idea how powerful and elite this bank
is!
In 2015 Google reported a staggering 74.5 Billion in Revenue with a total market capitalization of 373
Billion
Dollars!! Do you realize how INSANE that is??
Google ranks as the NUMBER ONE Internet Company and its Adsense Bank is the Wealthiest Bank on
Planet Earth!
Compare to the same year Bank of America chugged in at 15.8 Billion, and this is the bank that owns half the
real estate in America!
You get my drift.
In the movie The Social Network (Sony Pictures 2010) we see Napster CEO Sean Parker coerces Mark
Zuckerberg to
show up at a very important meeting with Capital Investors in bathrobe and flip flops.
Though I love the movie (I am a huge Z-berg fan) I think this part in particularly did more damage to
entrepreneurs than the producers intended it to.
Zuckerberg is a work horse, he does not lounge around in a bathrobe and flip flops eating potato chips and
playing video games. Sean Parker had to convince Zuckerberg to dress this way only way to convince the
investors that he was a busy man that didn't need their money. It was a risky gamble, but it worked to their
benefit.
HOWEVER Mark Zuckerberg had built and patented his machine- it was called Facebook and the investors knew
exactly what it would do.
YOU have NOT built your machine YET, so you better walk into that bank looking like you have!
Zuckerberg did not get rich fast, he worked his butt off to make Facebook what it is today.
Sadly I think many aspiring entrepreneurs saw the Silicon Valley era of new millionaires as the goofy college
kids that were throwing darts at Wall Street, trying to lure investors.
That's not true. Investors are smart... (really smart) and the investors that helped fund Facebook are the same
investors that share stock in The Bank of Google.
So please, have your documents and paperwork filled out neatly and correctly because you are not only applying
for a gracious loan but for the privilege of working with the single most profitable and equitable financial
institution in the world.

Hey Wait... Am I really applying for a Loan?

Yes you are! (In Fred G Sanford Voice) "Ya Big Dummy!!"

Don't get your feelings hurt. I was once a big dummy too, but the nice part is you won't be a big dummy for

long- not after reading this book.

Behind the large vaulted doors at the back of the foyer in the Bank of Google lobby, there is a red sign that

says:

"Private Access Only"

There is a hallway behind those doors that lead to a massive, stadium sized building that houses the Youtube

Machine.

For every square inch of ground around the machine, there are markers with numbers that designate "Lots".

These real estate lots are tiny parcels of land that people set up their machines on and hook up to the giant

Youtube machine.

These little lots are ridiculously expensive, and cost a small fortune just to own a tiny space.

They are so expensive in fact, that only the wealthiest people can afford to have big booths with lots of fancy

machines. There are normal people that are not rich with small booths and maybe one or two machines, but they

do not last long. In fact, the average person only spends about a year or so, tinkering around with their little machines before they either go broke or become frustrated.

Unfortunately there has never been a patented design for these machines that would make it easy for normal

people to make them work... until now. You have it in your hands.

Similar to the movie "The Social Network" you are pitching your idea to the Loan Consultants to try and raise

money to build your machine.

The loan consultants take your application and submit it to "venture capitalists" who review it and make a

decision or "bet" that you are a smart person with good business sense.

They figure if they are willing to make a small bet on you, that it may be a good return on investment. After

all, they will get a cut of everything your machines make.

As with traditional loans, there are different categories for the type of loan you will receive.

In traditional banks they have high risk loans and low risk loans. Since you are totally new to this bank and

have little or no money to start with, they are going to give you a "high risk loan."

This is kind of bad for you. But you gotta take what you can get. Beggars can't be choosers, and hey, at least they were willing to give you the loan in the first place! Not bad for a bank that doesn't even check your credit! The Google Bank is pretty generous, but like most banks, if you screw them over they can make your life

miserable (as you'll see later on.)

The details of this "High Risk Loan" are laid out in the simplest terms so that even poor, uneducated people

know what they are getting into.

The terms go something like this:

By accepting this loan from the Bank of Google, you are agreeing to the rules and regulations assigned by the

capital investors.

1. You must keep your real estate (booth space) outside the Youtube Machine clean at all times. No trash or

littering is allowed. If you allow your booth space to become dirty, we will make you disconnect your machines

for three months. After three months we will let you reconnect your machines. If after re-connecting your

machines your booth becomes unsightly or trashy again, we may cancel this loan indefinitely and you will be

required to remove your machines and booth from the premises.

2. Your machines must be serviced regularly and cause no damage to other machines or the main Youtube Machine.

Please ensure your machine is compatible with the list of machines we allow to be used. If your machine is not

compatible it will be removed and your loan may be canceled indefinitely.

If it sounds scary, it's because it is. You need to walk on pins and needles for a while until the Bank of Google sees you as a trustworthy member of its association.

But don't get too scared, because remember when you were in the Google Bank lobby with a fresh haircut, in

business attire with your documents in order? You were already in the right frame of mind because you respect

this financial institution and you understand how important it is to make a good first impression.

But don't forget about the people behind you that were wearing flip flops and bath robes, unshaven or hair in

curlers... those people will most definitely be the first to get their loans revoked by the Bank of Google. They probably didn't belong in this industry to begin with, there are plenty of other jobs more suitable for

them, but this is not one.

They are different than you. You are serious and eager to be successful... they are not.

Okay, here comes the technical part. Suprisingly this was the most difficult part of this book to write. The
only reason being that how you start these machines from the ground up, has a LOT to do with how successful you
will be. It's the difference between becoming a millionaire and stuffing this book on a shelf and saying "It didn't work for me."
Without further ado;
Creating Your Channels
My philosophy hinges on the 10 channel rule. So guess what? You're going to make 10 channels. Right from the
beginning.
Don't do any of this yet, wait until I begin the step-by-step process and follow it.
You will only be servicing and creating content for one channel to start off, but you still need to create 10
generic channels with generic titles.
These 10 channels will represent the bones of your machines that you will later use to clone your first machine.
To be more efficient, I'd create each channel by using your name sequentially like so:
Abe's Channel 1
Abe's Channel 2
Abe's Channel 3
Abe's Channel 4
Abe's Channel 5
Abe's Channel 6
Abe's Channel 7
Abe's Channel 8
Abe's Channel 9
Abe's Channel 10
Start by creating the first and go to the next, and follow the order until you are done. Don't even think about
modifying Channel 1 until all the channels have been created.
Don't worry about the generic titles, you will change them later after you've established your business plan.
Before you begin Step 1...
You will need to create ONLY ONE Google Account with a Gmail address. Even though you may already have a
personal Gmail account, all of your machines (channels) need to be housed under ONE GMAIL ACCOUNT. It needs to
be used only for dealing with business related to your channels.
Example: AbesChannels@gmail.com

Step 1

Once you have created an entirely new Gmail account, you can then proceed to the next step.
Start by going to Google Plus create a Page:
https://business.google.com/create
At the Create Page Menu choose "Brand"
Select Next and Here is Where you'll enter your first Generic Title:
Example: Abe's Channel 1
In the "Type" Drop Down Menu select: Entertainment
Click Create Page.
You should get a screen that says; Welcome to Google Business
Complete the New Page prompts until you have arrived at the Profile page for your new business.

Attention, before going further
REPEAT STEP 1 TEN TIMES UNTIL YOU HAVE 10 NEW BUSINESS PAGES
Label the pages Systematically [Example Abe's Channel 1 -- Abe's Channel 10]

Step 2
Sign-In to Youtube with your business email address: AbesChannels@gmail.com
Go to the Youtube Channel Switcher by entering this address in the search bar:
youtube.com/channel_switcher
There you will see all your Business Page Accounts.
Select the first one [i.e.; Abe's Channel 1]
You will see a popup that says Create Youtube Channel for Abe's Channel 1
Click "OK"

Attention, before going further
REPEAT STEP 2 TEN TIMES UNTIL YOU HAVE 10 NEW YOUTUBE CHANNELS

Congratulations on creating the bones of your first machines.
You should see under the Youtube Switcher landing page, a list of all ten Channels.
This is now what I will refer to as your portfolio.
These 10 channels are like 10 unique and different stocks. Every time you upload a new video to each channel
you are creating 1 share.
Every day, these shares will attract views, which are buyers. The more buyers for your shares, the higher your
stock will go up.
Memorize this metaphor until you see your channels and videos like stocks and shares.
The more shares (videos) you add to each stock (channel), the more money you make.
It's very simple.
On behalf of the International Digital Media Corporation of Independent Content Creators, I'd like to welcome
you to the largest money making enterprise of the 21st Century.

You are joining the ranks of hundreds of thousands of the world's richest entrepreneurs.

Awesome! When do we apply for our loan?
All in good time, young grasshopper.
If you took your bare bones machines with you into the loan department, they wouldn't be impressed. Right now
all you have are desktop computer shells with hard-drives, memory and a video card- basically just enough to
make them boot when you press the power button.
You will need to install a processor in each of these machines, which is no easy task.
By now you need to be asking yourself what kind of processor you want to put in these machines. This is a
loaded yet intimate question that only you can answer. I will give you my recommendations based on what kind of
personality you have, what time commitments you can make and even how much energy you have to invest. But don't
let this deter you, the blueprints are all here. Think of it like a franchise, there are plenty of franchise businesses I will offer you, you will know right away if it suits you are not.
The next chapter details these processors in such great length that it ensures not only the survival of your
business but the long term infrastructure to make you exceedingly wealthy.
Once our processors are selected we will put them into our machines (Chapter 3) and proceed with the next step
(Chapter 4) which is getting our loan approved!

Chapter 4
Choosing the Right Processor

This chapter is most near and dear to my heart for the intimate relationship I've shared with sales and marketing for the past 15 years.

I cut my teeth on Seth Godin's books as a senior in highschool, and by the time I had been promoted to marketing manager of Comcast's West Division sales affiliate; Paramount Marketing, I had put Godin's "Permission Marketing" (2001) at the top of new hire's required reading list.

Kids; there isn't any shortcut around a balanced education in successful marketing, sorry.

In the stampede of terror following the aftermath of Phil Defranco's video alerting his fan base that Youtube was shutting down Monetization for certain videos, he jokingly remarked; "I guess we'll all have to go get real jobs now."

Though this actually may be a reality for creators oblivious to white-hat optimization; it certainly opened a subjective chasim for angry teenage camera queens to pepper bullets into.

Maybe I'm too presumptious but I think Youtube just dropped a gold nugget for colleges everywhere offering anything to do with sales. Kids are going to have to go school; at least for a few semesters if only to learn that advertising campaigns aren't tiny boxes you check on your Adsense account.

Or, they can do what any able bodied salesperson with no college money does and stockpile Seth Godin's library of marketing witchcraft because you're going to need all the magic you can get.

A favorite quote of mine was Seth's prediction on literary marketing;

"The future of publishing is about having connections to readers and the knowledge of what those readers want."

The same is true for video and video creators. Youtube knows this; Caveat; Hollywood and big media knows this.
Everyone knows it!

The way you make money (and lots of it) is by connecting with your viewers. If your viewers are illegally stealing content then you should resort to legal proceedings, if that doesn't work- try advertising (sorry that was a lame joke.)

Advertising has worked for a little bit until Ad execs saw the videos that were attracting the most views. It wasn't that Ad Execs were trying to shutdown free speech, it was because the videos most in demand were promoting really terrible slanderous behavior. Some of it was just mentally unhealthy (i.e. fights, fueds, bullying, trolling) but the line was drawn where controversial, slanderous or damaging dialogue was directly or indirectly attacking companies and the reputation of the nation.

Journalists say this is freedom of expression. Youtube agrees and chooses to allow the videos to stay online.

It was almost another win for the money moochers, but in August of 2016 Time published a ticking time bomb:
"Why We're Losing the Internet to the Culture of Hate."

Yikes.

But I don't even think the children of the 2016 video bubble even subscribed to the Times. Maybe they should've, because it would've given them a heads up their channels were about to implode.

You see, the Times like all other traditional media agencies once played by the rules and actually new what an Advertising Campaign meant (you know the Madmen guys that took Advertising Executives out to wine and dine?)

So the Ad Execs and the producers, the film makers -all the traditional media guys are looking around and saying; "what are we doing wrong?"

The Times knew. And blew the whistle; bad behaviour is being rewarded.

Enter the Ad Execs that are getting looted like a drunk old man behind a department store while consumer confidence is plummeting and alternative news is fueling coup d'etat sentiment while lining their pockets.

I mean, it got really, really bad.

At some point I think the big brains got together and realized they were being taken from all sides.

If the FBI can't bust down every suburban door for every IP address clocking illegal movie streaming and the Supreme Court is sort of sitting on the fence with their hands in the air, what do you do?

Fair Use Act? Fine. Illegal file sharing? Fine. Free Music Videos? Fine.

Profiting from extorting and exploiting news that damages our reputation? Sorry! Your card's been declined.

But the game is not over. Youtube is just going to stop rewarding bad behavior and start rewarding the people that take the time to go to school and learn what an Advertising Campaign actually is.

It means regulation but that also means job creation in all the right places.

So yeah, maybe go to school for a while... or buy some good books.

Another marketing must-read is Brian Kramer's book;Shareology: How Sharing Is Powering the Human Economy (2015). A powerful perspective on the human connection and the intellectual "gifts" we share with one another.

The human side of the Youtube machine is driven by many things, but understanding the positive ways that we contribute to this evolution of thought, data and content are paramount. Kramer makes a valuable connection to this phenomena in how human relationships are being forged and creating a dynamic marketing environment.

In 2015 I wrote a letter to President Barack Obama, expressing a thought that came to me regarding a portion of his autobiography. In it I mentioned how small our intentions can seem even when broadcasted from the roof tops. "Many people may hear what we are saying but only a handful may make the connection" (I said this because I felt a key part of his book had been overlooked and for all my searching could not find anyone else that had honed in on this reflection that I found very powerful) and wrote; "I hear you loud and clear.""

Two months later he returned a scribbled note; "I'm honored. Thanks for Sharing."

It never ceases to amaze me how significant these seemingly small connections are that we make every day.

Many content creators are learning that the best strategy above anything is sharing deeply personal insights that viewers can connect with.

Though the strategy behind building "fast processors" for your machines is based on the most popular content categories, remember that YOU are the person behind the story. It is your unique perspective that will really make the difference.

Now that you have ten bare bones machines, I want you to take out a sheet of paper or create a word document
and list all ten of them in order.
What I am going to have you write down are the most optimal processors for your channels.
If at all possible purchase a large white board to hang on your wall so you can have more control over the
day-today dynamics of how these channels evolve. Write the list of your 10 channels on the whiteboard the same

as you would on the paper or word document.

Out of the list I provide below, circle the categories you think are most interesting to you (pick at least 5)

Biographies (i.e.; Mark Twain Memoirs)

History (i.e.; Civil War)

Health (i.e.; Natural Cures)

Spirituality (i.e.; Esoteric Mysteries)

Business and Finance (i.e.; Cryptocurrencies)

Cultural/Social Issues (i.e.; Black Entrepreneurs)

Children/Learning (i.e.; Book and Game Reviews)

Pop Culture (i.e.; Celebrities and Gossip)

Food (i.e.; Vegan Raw Cooking)

Romance (i.e.; Honeymoon Destinations)

Once you've identified your 5 favorite categories, write them under the top five channels on your paper in the

order they are of most interest to you.

These are the highest attractors of viewership in the world. They are like steroids for you channel and they

work all year round. Centralizing your channel around these categories gives you a head start above everyone

else. Note: You may make a channel outside these categories, for instance "Pets" but I don't guarantee they

will work within this system. I have never tested them and cannot attest to how well they optimize traffic.

Now that you have your 5 categories listed in order, find a sub category in each of those 5 categories; Example:

History: Civil War, The Egyptians, Atlantis, The Unsolved Ancient Wonders

Biographies: Great Inventors, New Age Visionaries, Wealth Gurus

Food: Vegan, Gluten Free, Paleo Diet, Bio Hacks

Spirituality: Myths and Legends, Magic, Biblical Expose

Cultural/Social Issues: Ethnic Progressivism, Non-binary Gender, Zionism

Once you have identified 5 sub-categories that peek your interest, put them into the next column.

Your 10 categories should look something like this (Notice at the end of #5 I started back at the top with my

subcategories for 6-10) :

1.   Food

2.   Spirituality

3.   Romance

4.   Health

5.   Biographies
6.   Vegan Athletic
7.   Esoteric Folklore
8.   Finding Love Strategies
9.   Natural Remedies
10.   Ancient Civilizations

Great! You have now identified the business plans for each of these channels. These are your processors and
these are what will power your machines.
These two websites should be the well-worn tools in your content creator's hand bag:
google.com/trends/
google.com/trends/correlate
These two, very easy to use websites are like pure gold, and nearly every media outlet uses them.
When you wake up in the morning you should check these sites within the context of your categories to track what's making waves.

Refrain from broadcasting the same story across all channels. This is not only against Youtube's rules but against lucrative marketing strategies.

To quote best selling author and Marketing strategist Joe Pulizzi;

"The easiest way to turn off your community members is to broadcast the same message across multiple channels. Instead, determine the kind of content that interests the members of your community in a way that is useful to them."

-From "Content Inc.: How Entrepreneurs Use Content to Build Massive Audiences and Create Radically Successful Businesses 2015"

Another hot tip is to use Twitter to search emerging trends in your categories. Twitter can often latch on to
trends faster than Google Trends based on its organic social sharing algorithm.
Either way, the system is quite simple.
You have your ten business plans that tell you what type of content you are going to generate every day for
each channel. And for each channel you have the Google Trends and Twitter to research new emerging topics as
they are trending.
You couldn't ask for an easier way to make yourself wealthy beyond your wildest dreams!

But there is a faster way (The secret that all the most successful Youtube Channels have already learned)

The super-duper fast processor I use for my channels is....

NEWS! Political News! Celebrity News! it doesn't matter as long as it's outrageous and SENSATIONAL.

Understand that care needs to be taken to leverage both the exciting nature of news yet tread lightly when the
controversy can turn off advertisers from using your channel to market their products.

Have you ever walked into a Supermarket and noticed the Enquirer, Gossip Magazines etc. are situated right next
to the candy, drinks and snacks? The one thing these products have in common is their ability to manipulate the
impulse of the buyer.
Though I will teach you to tap into the impulse nature of any category you have chosen by creating momentum in
your products, sensational news needs no momentum!
Sensational news creates its own momentum, it's like a hot stock that everyone is buying. You want that stock
in your portfolio (if at the very least, one of your stocks needs to be a hot stock!)
Every hot story you can find needs to be funneled into your "hot stock" channel.
The reason ALL OF MY CHANNELS are NEWS related channels is because I only deal in hot stocks!
Every day my videos attract thousands of viewers simply because the news is generating its own momentum.
Harness the power of that news and it will make your machines pump like a twin turbine engines.

But don't take my word for it. Only you can learn by testing the waters in your own strategy.

For the many people reading this book there are undoubtedly (and with good reason) more than a handful that
will find chasing news to be too exhausting of a venture.
It's true, it can and will wear you down if you let it.
If you feel like sensational news is either not your cup of tea (or safe for your mental or spiritual wellbeing) then please use the rest of this chapter to get acquainted with creating momentum in your selected
categories.
The categories I showed you are prime stocks. They do well, consistently year after year after year.
You will still need to know how to create entertaining content (and quality content.)

We will get into how to increase the momentum of your non-news products and then return to sensational news at
the end of the chapter.

Generating Momentum

Selling a product is not difficult when the demand is high, but you will still need to present it in a way that
makes it irresistible for customers.

Despite the health conscious news about sugar, saturated fat and calories etc., consumers are increasingly
buying more snack foods and candy every year.

Most treats are in snack size portions and are relatively cheap. To make these devilish pleasures even more
irresistible, grocery chains place them near the checkout counters where customers make rash decisions. You may
wonder why the checkout area differs from other places in the store and why customers become more impulsive in
this location; the answer is pretty simple- the customer is rushing to get out of the store. They also have a
limited opportunity to satisfy a whim craving before they pay for their purchases and make the long commute
home.

Suppliers of these snacks and candies understand the mighty power of the "impulse buyer".

Flat screen TV's and flashy new cars are both expensive commodities that are surprisingly lumped into impulsive
sectors of retail. Many new car owners make purchases after casually strolling onto new car lots with never
intending on buying. Every effort is made to leverage the ease of loan approval, relaxed environment and legal
paperwork to put a customer into a car before they second-guess themselves.

Manufacturers of snacks and candies have learned that if you make a product in smaller quantities you can sell
it for cheaper prices, creating less resistance in decision. They pull all stops to keep momentum going and you
need to do the same for your products.

Building momentum is an art, but there are some simple formulas to make it easier. There are Youtube channels
that use the "Countdown system" of labeling certain things in order; i.e. "The 10 Worst Presidents in History."
People will stick around to watch the video just to see who the absolute worst one is.

You can use this strategy in your everyday videos in a similar way. Creating a video that says; "This Friday I
have a special surprise for you!" will naturally pique the interest of return viewers to find out what it is.
But don't stop there- you need to build momentum all the time, in every possible way that you can. This is the

difference between "bland" products and "delicious" products.

Mister Rogers put the educational parts of his famous TV show at the beginning of every episode. At the end, as

a reward for "sticking it through" he would whisk you away on the trolley to the Neighborhood of Make-Believe.

The brutish "Man Show" that once aired on Comedy Central with Adam Corolla and Jimmy Kimmel used "girls

bouncing on trampolines" at closing credits to keep their male viewers engaged 'till the end.

You need to develop a strategy for not only weekly momentum, but daily and even "to-the-minute" momentum.

That sounds exhausting. How can I build momentum every minute?

It's really not as hard as it sounds. Momentum can also be measured by the speed at which your product is being delivered to the customer. Take for instance the "QVC" Home shopping network; they often have a countdown timer that squeezes the customer into a short decision period. Buy or Die! You can only buy this sweater in the next 10 minutes, and supplies are limited! You will notice they also advertise how many sales are being made and announce when supplies have been exhausted;

"We're sorry, but we just sold the last sweater to caller 25."

This is generating momentum by creating a quick pace and the customer is being pressured to make a decision

within the allotted time.

You need to do the same exact thing with your product, and with a little practice you will eventually do it

without thinking about it.

Cutting out all the pauses and dead air with video editing software is ABSOLUTELY ESSENTIAL. A long winded

video has no momentum, and you will lose most interest within the first 60 second segment of your video (60

seconds if you're lucky!)

You are constantly pitching your product to your customer, that's right- PITCHING!

Every video is essentially an advertisement with Billy Mays giving his Oxyclean spill - "but hold on, there's

more!"

I don't expect you to act like a maniac to increase view count.

What you have to do is read between the lines of any trending news story to find a place to spin the story.

Some Channels like the Shaytards utilize the goofiness of unexpected improv in ordinary, every day situations.

Others like Jenna Marbles use comedy to break news, events and random topics down to the skit level.

Whatever you choose to do, make it uniquely you. There is something inside each of us that makes us different from the rest but that's an entirely different book.

Read Seth Godin's book "Purple Cow" to get a better understanding of what being remarkable means from a marketing perspective.

How many times have you visited a video that gave you the exact information you were looking for but was
delivered so dryly it pained you to watch it to the end?
Don't make your customers skip or fast forward through your videos. Keep the energy flowing, use your solution
as the bait at the end of the hook and then whisk them away on the trolley to the Neighborhood of Make-Believe.

Sensational News

What I like about sensational news is that hardly a day goes by that I can't find something trending to capitalize on.
Once upon a time, I was a slow mover and a slow investor.
I only thought in very linear terms when it came to how I was going to make my money.
Becoming a Day Trader had a lot to do with transforming that, because I begin to see the value in investments
that were dynamic and fluid.

Think of it like a time machine that speeds up the natural process of things by minutes, hours or days.

A slow stock may increase in value over time, but the time period is lengthy; hence the longer you will be
waiting to get rich.

A volatile stock may increase its value in half the time, increasing the time frame for making your fortune.

This method is risky for the day trader, because he must protect himself from risk because these highs and lows
directly affect
the compounding interest and loss rate of his investment.

But the beautiful thing about having a media portfolio is that your revenues do not compound negatively. There
is no reverse cycle
or "back flow" of the money in your Adsense accounts.

Here's where the small fish need to listen, because the Big fish are already in the know.
In traditional TV advertising, news channels like FOX News or CNN regularly adjust the cost of their advertiser
spots based on the nature of the news.

Have you ever heard the saying "Red Letter Day" or "Slow News Day?"

Both of those refer to the unique nature in which a media organization makes its money.
Back in the days of paper and print, when the New York Times relied on newsboys to peddle their media on the
streets, a slow news day
actually had a direct impact on their revenues for that day.
If there was nothing exciting or particularly sensational about the news that day, the peddlers couldn't give
their papers away.
But on Red Letter days, the newsprint media industry could count on their revenues going sky high!
As this system evolved they recognized a pattern and could predict with safe certainty the demand for their
product based on sensational news.
Once these financial peaks and valleys were structured into their accounting, the media moguls designed a
strategy to leverage it.
By charging advertisers more money on the Red Letter Days they could enhance their revenue shares across the
board.

As Advertising agencies evolved to further capitalize on profits made by media, they incorporated the same
strategies for television
by developing advertising campaigns for clients that diversified commercials over a range of hot spots.

Even today this system is used and has created its own virtual "Stock market Exchange" of buying advertising
spots sometimes
years ahead of popular events like the Super bowl.

Today a company can buy 100 advertising spots for an upcoming Super bowl and sell them to "media scalpers" at a
profit the closer
it gets to game day.

Don't start yawning now, because this is the difference between you being wealthy or reading "how to get
wealthy" books for the rest
of your life.

Even if you are a content creator that just wants to better your channels and strategy, this is key to your success.
Without understanding how advertisers pay for your Adsense spots or how "Prime Time TV" or "Red Letter Day"
affects your
window of opportunity to send content to your channels, you won't get ahead.

Part of the job that you as a media mogul must accept is that without slanting or spinning the news to your
benefit; you don't have a story at all. Few people will read the same regurgitated story more than once. The
big news media corporations already know this
and they bid with their dollars for Google to give them top priority in the News Feed.

What you have to do is come up with a new way to spin the sensational story.
Now most of you have already caught on to this, so for the pro's my only advice is to think about the
advertisers when spinning your story. In Chapter 1 we talk about how stories can hurt advertisers, so if you
want to monetize but think it might be a bit too controversial it probably is.

Creating hype where hype doesn't exist is something you must practice until it becomes second nature.

It's sort of like going to an Improv class where you have to think on your feet and react to the people around
you in a creative way.
People that are good at Improv are inherently good at acting, because they can get into character and feed into
the momentum.
Bad Improv actors will only absorb the momentum without sending the energy back out.

That is what you must refrain from doing in all of your news stories.
You must refrain from letting your emotional and mental energy become absorbed by the momentum building in the
news story.

Example:

A shooting has just happened somewhere in Paris and little information is known. The events are unfolding and
the story is dynamic.
It may seem heartless and cruel, but media organizations all over are actively researching the story to see if
it has
the necessary qualities to be a front page story. If it turns out to be a quarrel between two lovers, the story
might as well be dead
in the water. Nobody will follow the story to read about a shooting between two estranged love birds. However if the shooting is claimed by a rogue group of criminal dissidents, it could sprout wings and fly.

Good guy/Bad Guy, Red Team/Blue Team, Democrat/Republican has been played so well that the media has to do very
little to make
the metrics of their big processors work. It practically works on its own with very little intervention.

Window of Opportunity

To the side of my desk I have a large wall sized dry-erase board.
My mornings usually begin at 4:30 a.m. and I am showered, dressed and coffee made by 5:00 a.m.
My desk is spotless, except a small stack of yellow sticky notes, a pen and highlighter.
No matter what kind of news day it is, I will always be able to find one sensational story to get started.
Here is where I am going to give you another of my personal secrets; my top five highest traffic channels.
They are Business, Sports, Politics, Celebrity Gossip and Health.
Out of these categories I am never out of work, there is always something moving here that I can find to spin a story. On slow days I try to fill out the lower categories that are not "heavy hitters" in terms of traffic. Each time I pick a story I want to capitalize on, I fill out a sticky note with the main topic points and place it in the proper category on the white board.

Once this is done, the sticky note will remain at the top of the category in a row labeled "pending"

(I have ten columns and 3 rows, so it looks sort of like a checkerboard)

When I have begun production of the video, I move the yellow sticky note into the "production" row.

When the video is complete I move it into the "Live" row.

This final row lets me visually see that my video is now live on the web and ready for monetization.

For me, this system worked the best and helped me stay organized and mentally engaged on the right projects.

At the level I work at now, I do not create any content at all. But when I first started, I would do all of the content creation, video editing, voice over and uploading.

Right now all I do is come up with the story and write scripts.

In the beginning it would take me on average 2 to 3 hours from start to finish to make a video.
When I had streamlined the system, I gradually worked myself out of a job and passed the lengthier parts of
the video editing off to a freelancer (we discuss this in a later chapter; hiring workers.)
Don't start crying because you can't afford to outsource people, the road to 100,000 views per day comes
very fast, and eventually you will be able to eat the difference of a team of freelance content creators with a single good day of heavy traffic volume.

With ten channels to feed every week, I found it was easier to focus on two videos per day.

At a rate of three videos per day, I managed to hit my goal of getting roughly 15 to 18 videos created per week.
Again, don't get discourage if you are only getting one or two videos uploaded in a day.
Remember once these videos are created, they will continue to attract visitors, give them time- but don't stop
creating content. Youtube will reward your channel for being active and consistent by placing it in the higher
suggestion tiers.

Here is where it gets tricky; getting the hottest videos live on the web is the most stressful part of my day.
The window of opportunity to feed into momentum is very delicate. If you miss your window of opportunity,
it can often mean the difference of a few thousand views. And as you will begin to see with your own business,
when that five thousand views is spread over 10 channels, you are looking at a loss of 50,000 views per week.

There is no way to get around the hustle of meeting your deadlines for competitive news stories.
This will be the way you become a six figure media mogul, so you'll just have to learn to enjoy the fast paced life of trending news.

Many times when I am just checking out for the day at two in the afternoon, a headliner will catch fire and
I have to drop any dinner plans or evening activities to launch a new video.

After time this business starts to grow on you. You learn which stories to chase and which stories to leave
alone.

If I am ever on the move outside my home office, I never leave without my laptop. I can work from any location
(minus the whiteboard) and with a few strokes of the keyboard, whip out a 300-400 word script for voiceover
if I really need to. I try not to make this a habit, as I really value time with the family but if you ever
see me racing to the car for my laptop, it's probably because Twitter suddenly exploded.

For me a good story usually has 3 sensational elements:

1. The topic has been trending or consistently stayed in the headlines for more than two weeks

2. The topic is controversial, time sensitive or unfolding

3. The topic could impact or disrupt future events, legal proceedings, business sectors etc.

I don't stray far from these three golden rules. If I ever question the longevity of any particular story
I simply ask myself if it falls into at least one of these categories and if it doesn't, I don't chase it.

One of my favorite examples that includes the unfolding element was the passing of the Singer/Songwriter
legend Prince. On the day the news broke, I was monitoring Twitter for any significant branch outs of
information I could use for a story. Within the first thirty minutes, someone commented on the fact that
Prince's death was yet another eerie prediction depicted in Matt Groening's animated TV series "The Simpsons."
Right away I Google searched the video and used that as a critical part of my news story;
"Did the Simpsons Predict Prince's Death?" The video attracted 100,000 views in the first 48 hours.

As a caveat, this story took a bad turn when creators capitalized on speculation that Prince had overdosed.
The golden rule for me is that I never speculate on drugs, abuse or anything that could get my video de-monetized.

An example of how a story impacts future events is any critical piece of legislation passed by the senate

that could affect how certain sectors of business operate. In the case of Healthcare reform, there were many
niche health sectors like long term care facilities, Rehab centers and Nursing Homes that were directly impacted by changes to Medicare Plans. By creating the dialogue; "5 ways Medicare Plan B providers will be
impacted by new healthcare laws" I was able to direct nearly 300,000 viewers to my video.

What is most important about creating good content is ensuring your video asks the right questions.

The better you get at "future speculation" the better your content will be.

Future speculation is simply submitting a theory or problem before it has been suggested or perhaps asking it in a different way.

For instance, if Genetically Modified Foods is a hot button issue for Vegan or Raw food advocates, the news surrounding a new hybrid of wheat crop may not be an issue that makes it beyond agriculture trends.
But by asking; "Can Consumers Still buy Non-GMO Wheat?" is suggesting that there may be fewer and fewer ways for GMO conscious shoppers to avoid it. It is all how you present the story that makes the difference.

Though I hate to sound redundant, it is difficult to teach both the nature of good marketing (especially in relation to news media) and good advertising. Both would appear to play on the same team, but for Youtube purposes they don't. YOU are the marketer, viewers are the customers and Advertisers place the ads.

The above example referring to GMO foods is going to trigger Adsense keywords related to food distributors and the agriculture industry as well. Though this may be confusing, corporations like Monsanto and General Mills have close knit ties that rely on eachother in more ways than just supply chain. If your video is Anti-GMO (which would hurt Monsanto revenues) most likely General Mills would not want to advertise on your channel, presenting the real possibility your video may not be eligible for monetization.

To make this simple, just keep your advertisers in mind when creating content.

If you know a video will have controversial implications that could affect advertisers, don't monetize it. It's pretty simple stuff.

Chapter 5
You Don't Need a Camera

You read it right- you DON'T need a camera to have a successful Youtube channel. Sound like I'm going off the deep end? If you don't believe me go search Youtube for "Top5s" a channel with 1.5 Million Subscribers and an average of 600,000 views per video that uses no camera what-so-ever. The creator uses a voiceover to read an script in the classic "VH1" style of video presentation. A fast moving collage of photos with an "expert sounding" dialogue in the "History Channel fashion" creates the documentary illusion... but make no mistake, this is NOT a film... no cameras were harmed in the making of this video!

Slide presentation videos are actually outrageously popular, but so are other non-film related videos like "Music" videos. The #1 most watched video on Youtube is "Gangham Style by South Korean musician Psy."
Now I am not suggesting you get into the business of music videos. The reason "Gangham Style" has been watched so many times is not because it's is the revolutionary battle hymn of all free peoples- it's simply because it's a party song like "Thriller" by Michael Jackson (also among the top watched videos of all time.) Most millennials lacking a DJ service, be it at private parties or backyard weddings turn to Youtube to fetch their favorite party hits. Sadly, Psy and many other musicians do not benefit from the "drunk music binges" that drive these videos to hundreds of thousands of views. Often times the only person cashing in on these videos are lawless hacks or brash techies trying to make a quick buck. Don't rush to start making lyric videos with copyrighted songs playing in the background though, because Youtube will not pay out on videos lacking the proper content licensing (and they have a whole team of people who routinely monitor payments made to channels with suspiciously high volume.)

But cheer up buttercup, there is still plenty of money to be made on videos with music that you don't need licenses for. Classical music is one of them.

Labels
Though I strongly considered putting this part about labeling Videos in its own chapter, I decided to keep it embedded here because it is part of the same body of information. I don't want to lose you later on where you might not read this part in its entirety.
Yes, Labeling and tagging Videos is that Important.
There are thousands of paid workers around the world labeling and tagging everything from blog articles to Amazon products-- it is literally a million dollar industry and will soon be a billion dollar industry. Someone got the bright idea of labeling classical music videos with "Best Music to Study to" which naturally leads hundreds of thousands of college students to these videos at the height of finals every semester.
Labels are small and seemingly unimportant to the novice Youtuber, but they are like the billboards of the internet highway. Anyone that has taken a road trip knows how vital those illuminated signs are at night.

Whether it's a hotel, gas station or nearest fast food joint, they stand out from the landscape and point you to tiny buildings you might not even see from the road.

Your Youtube videos are like little gas stations or hotels that are mostly invisible from the drivers' vantage point. Your viewers are zooming across the internet expressway looking for indications that a business is selling what they're looking for. Your gas station may be the best in a 100 mile radius but if customers can't find it, you might as well file for bankruptcy.

When you create a label such as: "Relaxing Music to Sleep To" -you have just erected a massive billboard on the world wide web.

By adding tags or keywords like: "Chopin, Mozart, Bach, Cello, Symphony" you add the necessary road signs to get people off the highway and over to your business.

If you're reading this book, chances are you already use labels and keywords for you videos... that's fine, however, if you're reading this book it's also more likely your videos are not harnessing their competitive edge.

Example; in August of 2016 while the Republican Convention was being broadcasted over live TV, I was betting that millions of cable cutters (i.e.; non TV watchers) were going to be waiting for a live upload of Donald Trump's acceptance speech. Here was an opportunity to direct millions of customers looking for a specific product to my News Channel. All I had to do was use the key words: "Donald Trump Republican Nomination Acceptance Speech 2016" and embed that into one of my videos. I took a screenshot of the video live and used it for the cover photo of the video to make it more attractive. Now all I needed was a quick video detailing the event that took place and covering a few brief points from his speech and "Voila!" I had a prime "Billboard" to get millions of customers off the highway and over to my channel.

To be fair to my customers, I took a link of the actual video that was later uploaded by a local news affiliate and added it to my video as an Ad banner that said; "To See the Full Acceptance Speech, Click Here."

You see, even the local news affiliate did not take the time to do the proper tagging and labeling of their video. If my memory is correct their label was; "Trump RNC Speech WKNOA" and that kind of label is what refer to as "dead labeling."Dead labeling is just a generic title slapped on a video by some in-house tech goon that could care less about how many views it gets.

My video ended up getting 286,000+ views while the actual news affiliate's video got half of that (possibly even most of that was referral traffic from my video.) Labeling and tagging your videos is such an important key to your success, it is the last thing I'd outsource to another person.

Let's look at some more examples:

You know there is a going to be a big "Pay Per View" fight tonight, and you want to take advantage of the millions of customers searching the web to see or read about the highlights. By creating a video with the Label: "Rhonda Rousey Fight Pay Per View, October 2016" you've taken the first step to put your billboard up. Chasing news is both beneficial and detrimental, it's a double edged sword. Most of your customers will not stay more than a couple seconds if they perceive your video as nothing more than a "bait and switch" so you need to give them something meaty within the opening minute of your video. You need to provide a quality product to your customer; product, service or solution.

By creating your "Rhonda Rousey" video you can also add other tags or keywords like; "Epic knock out, last round or K.O." As the fight begins in real time, you need to be searching Youtube for any relevant videos related to the fight. Some people will upload camera phone videos of particular fight scenes. As a general rule, Youtube removes lengthy videos of Pay Per View fights, as it violates the content licensing laws that protect them. You are only looking for relevant information to add meat to your video. Pay per view is probably not the best example because there's so much legal implications involved.

I am not telling you to post illegal content, just helping you understand how capitalizing on content as it evolves real time, is the fastest way to attract viewers.

I want you to see the nature and habits of customers, what they are searching for and how they find your products. Following a gossip news site like TMZ is a great way to get tip offs to large groups of traffic across the internet highway.

There are plenty of ways to spin a story and build on momentum. TMZ may post a video on a Branjolina tiff and you could create a video with the label; "Did Brad Pitt just Dump Angelina Jolie?"

Chasing news will not make you rich; the customer traffic from it will not be your bread and butter subscriber base so learn to utilize this method only when building a channel from scratch.

What I'm trying to help you see is that each channel you create does not need to have your smiling face beaming at the world in every video. Each channel is a business, and each business offers an entirely unique product. As you begin to build these businesses from scratch and more customers come to your stores, you'll find it's much easier to "hire employees" to do the work for you. There are dozens of sites like Upwork and Fiver with technical professionals worldwide that can create content for you in just about any style, technique and even language. Their service fees range from Five dollars (hence the name "Fiver") to even bidding on prices YOU set (like Upwork.) Your goal at the higher tiers of business operations is to move from a single business owner to a multi-company Corporate Executive.

Even the research into niche markets on which to develop new channels (stores) can be outsourced to other people.

If you have ten channels with a subscriber base of just 30,000 each- you now have a combined 300,000 subscribers. With that kind of monthly income you could outsource a "content manager" to manage the "content creators". Let's not get ahead of ourselves, there is a lot left to learn- I just want you to understand how the majority of millionaires are making it big on Youtube.

You don't know their names and they aren't celebrities, they are just ordinary people operating multiple channels with hundreds of thousands of subscribers!

Multiple Channel Networks and Multiple Channel Partners

Though this subject is important, it is not something we will linger on for very long.

Multiple Channel Networks (MCN) and Multiple Channel Partners (MCP) are basically corporate brokers that take your channel, combine it with hundreds (i.e.; thousands) of other channels and then go to AdSense and other advertisers to negotiate higher advertising revenue. The brokers use this leverage to increase your sales every month and of course take a cut (percentage) of your sales.

The long and short of this is, YES this is something you want to do. On average I DOUBLE my daily revenue with MCNs! That is the difference between my channel making $50 a day and $100 a day.

But proceed with caution! Do not sign lengthy contracts. Even a year is too long. Look for companies that allow you to cancel your partnership at any time. There are also lots of scam agencies out there that do nothing but take a percentage of your profit, so do your research before jumping on the bandwagon.

Here are three that I recommend: Viso, Broadband and ScaleLab, as always by simply checking reviews of a company out on the web, you can quickly determine if a company is legit or not.

Some may argue that they are fine with signing long-term contracts, and that is an option only you will be able to determine is right for you.

My channels are my business and I am a huge control freak when it comes to stuff like this.

Be advised that at the time this book was written, the advice to use MCNs or MCPs was based on the assumption that there still non-contract based firms to work with.

Increasing views on slow movers or dead videos

You need to be consistently monitoring your slow moving or dead videos. It is far easier to retool a rusty video than to make a new video from scratch.

There are two ways to spark ignition under the hood:

1: Change the Thumbnail of your video
2: Change the Title and Description of your video
Voila! Super easy.

Important note: let's say one of your videos is about Space Flight. Your view count has been slow and you've never changed anything since you created it. You finally decide to go in and change the thumbnail and description and all of the sudden your views shoot through the roof. There is an explanation for this, and many times it has nothing to do with your description or thumbnail at all (you'll find editing these things do not have the same effect for every video.)

Often by editing the video, crawlers will see the revised edit as new activity on the video and arrange it at the top of the search engine with newly minted videos.

This is particularly useful when an event or trending subject ties in with the video you just edited.

So maybe your Space Flight video wasn't popular when you made it two weeks ago, but since then NASA has released a press release about new flight initiatives. Now that you've edited your video the crawlers will collate your video on the trending subject of space flight.

Words of advice though, don't tamper too much with videos that are working. The same effect could decrease your view count on a video that is bringing you consistent revenue.

Knowing that some of my readers have never used Youtube prompted me to add a section in the "Tool bag" chapter. It is the more technical parts of the strategy you'll need to refer to in the future.

Though you will not be filming yourself talking, you will be taking videos from other places such as ABC, Fox News, TMZ or even popular nightly shows like Larry King or Jimmy Fallon.

In the Tool bag, I also cover at great length the copyright laws, fair use, and how to properly cite your videos so that you can use these third party videos legally and ethically.

In the Hiring Workers chapter, I talk about hiring people to act in your video in lieu of paying someone to read your script. I have found that paying someone to read a script into a microphone costs just about the same amount as paying someone to videotape themselves reading the words out loud. Ultimately you must make the decision as to how the flow of the video works from a viewer's perspective.

What has made me successful with content creation is breaking my process of creating non-filmed videos into a step by step process.

I follow this with just about every video I make.

1. Writing the Script.

2. Reading the script into a microphone (Voice Over)

3. Selecting videos and pictures to use in your slideshow

4. Combining the Voiceover (or Actor's video) with your slideshow presentation into a media file.

There are hundreds of software programs that turn a slideshow into a movie that can be uploaded to Youtube. Kizoa for instance is a Free Online Movie maker, however you will find that many of these movie makers put a watermark on their movie that cannot be removed.

Animoto is another option and one that I used primarily when I first started. It has a monthly subscription fee but really easy to use and I think it has the most professional interface possible for novices.

Another option that I hope you will use, instead of trying to collect multiple videos and images off the web to use for your news story, is a Screen Capture or Screen Recorder program like ScreenCastify (my favorite.)

Screencastify allows me to speak into a microphone while it records my desktop.

I can easily create all the tabs for my websites in order, in my browser.

This is really important for me, because most of my videos are very dynamic and fluid.
I can quickly switch from tab to tab, and play videos showing news stories while speaking into the microphone.

This enables me to read my script and show videos at the same time, and it actually makes the video seem a little more intimate verses putting together a static slideshow presentation.

If you use a screen recorder program, it also cuts out all of the video editing (like copying and pasting different videos into your content timeline.) It just makes it a lot easier, and I think you'll like it if you give it a try.

For example, I start the screen recorder and begin recording my desktop movements.
On my desktop I have a background with my Logo and channel information. (this saves me from making an intro)

My Video starts with me saying "Hi guys! I found this interesting News story today about a weird insect-like organism that is eating people's brains! It's called a Brain-Eating Amoeba and it lurks in ponds, rivers and oceans. Creepy right? Well that's not all, check out this article here"

(At this point I may pull up a window with an article that talks about it)

I click around and show a video that I have preselected in my tabs and push the play button.

At the end of my video, I add a closing statement like;

"So that's just a quick update for you, I'll keep you posted if I find out anything more about it."

The end.

You don't need to have a fancy intro and outro in every video! You just don't. Not with sensational media.
Be open, honest, straightforward and transparent; viewers like that.

Even if you outsource the voiceover to someone else, make sure you select a candidate that can read your script
in the way you intended it to be read.

One of the things I like to do is add a sarcastic poem or comical antidote at the end of my videos because
it makes people laugh and making people laugh seems to increase my subscribers.

When I make videos I want people to feel like they're getting their news from a trusted friend that has a funny personality.

Funny personality + Sensational News is like pure gold.

Just do it, over and over.

If you need inspiration on how to be funny and read the news, watch people like Stephen Colbert, Jimmy Fallon
or Jimmy Kimmel.

Watch how they pitch the news in quizzical, sarcastic undertones. Make notes and practice often.

The reason I mention the guys above, is because they have a unique way of spinning the news without wrecking advertiser ratings. However, there is a reason they are typically on the "Night shift" if you catch my drift. Advertisers can relax a bit because the majority of their viewer base is sleeping. Night shows tend to play the cards a bit more aggressively than day news, yet they still have to follow the same rules. That's why I HIGHLY RECCOMEND you pay attention to what these people talk about every night. Even if current events aren't your "thing" you will really benefit from keeping up to date on trending topics by tuning in to their broadcasts.

Chapter 6
Your Loan is Approved!

Some of you will think I'm scary crazy for suggesting you wait 90 days to turn monetization on for your channels, so let me explain.

Going back to the Bank of Google with a fully functional, fully operational portfolio of ten channels with a solid business plan is the only way to win at this game.

If you have followed the plan to the letter, you will know that I suggest 10 videos per week (or producing two videos per day) giving us a combined 120 videos at the time we turn on monetization for our channels.

If you have done this, you can thank me now.

Because you now see how fast your views calculate across the board. You should be rightfully proud. Even if each video only receives 500 views that's 60,000 views at the time you submit your application.

Why is this so important?

Believe it or not, even with a mere 60,000 views, Google can quickly calculate the metrics into it's monetization algorithm and get a much clearer snapshot of what your business looks like. There is also a short period where an actual human looks over your account to ensure it meets the guidelines for monetization.

Your view count and the overall professionalism of how your videos are posted, work like a virtual credit score used to rate your channel when Adsense turns on Monetization.

Adsense will not tell you any of these secrets, in fact very few people know about them. Little is known about the backend application of how Adsense deals it's dough.

You may hear a few folks try and convince you in their books or videos that they can break the CPM/CPC code, but the reality is- nobody knows how the bank rates channels.
The only thing I know, and I can guarantee you, is that Adsense gives a credit score to your account based on a perceived level of Integrity.

This is why it is so important to start this program from scratch with a completely new account. Your other channels outside of the ten we have created in this strategy, may or may not have a direct bearing on the integrity rating of your channels.

For instance, if you have a music or movie channel with some questionable content (i.e.; copyright license issues) your personal channel may affect your business channels.

With that said, if your channels have the appropriate licensing (with the licenses or notices placed correctly in the description) if your channels explicitly outline the educational nature of subjective journalism and name the collaborators that worked on the video (or in the case that the only collaborator is you- names the news channels; ABC, MSNBC, Associated Press etc. that you borrowed your videos from) then the loan approval department will see all of this and give you a much HIGHER CREDIT SCORE.

You see, the only thing Adsense lets us look at from a Monetization standpoint, is what advertisers are paying per click (or per impression etc.,) the view counts, ads blocked and so forth.

However, your hands are completely tied and your eyes are blindfolded to how it rates your channel in relation to the view count.

You are only trusting that Adsense is being transparent by telling you that "X" amount of subscribers did or didn't see your ad for "X" amount of time.

It never dawns on anyone that Adsense may levy restrictions on a percentage spread based on how it rates the integrity of your channel.

If I have confused you, here is an example:

You and your friend Billy both start media businesses and you both start out with 10 channels. You replicate the same system and follow virtually the same pattern for creating content.

However, Billy may have a personal Youtube channel that has copyrighted music playing in the background and it weakens his credit score when he goes to apply for an Adsense account.

You do not have any channels other than 10 media channels you and Billy built together.

At the time you and Billy start monetization, your stats are just about tied for viewer count and subscribers. Even your CPM/CPC rates are the same and you have the same advertiser list.

In the first week Billy notices his profits are on average 10-20% less than your revenue.

He modifies his CPC rates and even blocks advertisers that pay out smaller amounts for each impression/click.

Nothing changes; he is still making 10-20% less than your channel, regardless of what he does.

You both realize that Billy must have a lower integrity rating for his channel.
Billy then remembers he has a personal channel with questionable content on it and erases the channel/videos.

Three months later, Billy starts to see his revenue increase until finally, his percentages are closer in line with yours.

That would be a hypothetical example, there is no real way to test this because you can't copy other videos in their entirety and expect not to have your account flagged or possibly suspended for breaking the rules.

Just trust me when I say that being professional and taking the time to correctly label and "cite your sources" will pay off in the long run. Oh yeah- and if you DO have a personal Youtube Channel you should probably look it over a few times and ask yourself it it's worth risking suspension or even getting banned indefinitely.

For new users of Youtube I have put the step by step guide to turning on Monetization in the Toolbox section of this book.

If you are not ready to start monetization yet, continue reading and refer to the Toolbox when you need it.

Monetization is done now what?

I'm going to quote talented blogger/author Johnny B Truant in the context of an article he wrote on CopyBlogger;

How to Do 500 Times Better than AdSense:

"[Adsense]is not a business model. Any time you can talk about "monetization," you're probably not talking about a real business because "monetizing" a business is redundant. "Monetizing" is slapping a moneymaker on top of something that doesn't naturally produce income. The way that 99.99% of people dive into AdSense, they're simply putting something out there and waiting for the dollars to roll in. There is no real planning, no accounting forecasts, no intention down the road to improve workflow or expand offerings or enlarge the sales funnel, no exploiting the best abilities of yourself and partners to create benefit for others."

I suggest you read not only the article in its entirety but paste Johnny's blog to your forehead or any other kind of mind meld conditioning you may know of to sync brain waves with this guy. He's a genius.

Also, check out his publishing ventures at : sterlingandstone.net
But back to Adsense, Johnny is right.

Adsense is only a banking mechanism owned and operated by the bank of Google.

That is why this book is not built on decoding or deciphering Adsense CPC any other nonsense.
Blocking low paying advertisers will only marginalize viewer success rates, period.

You have to see your content portfolios as a branch of the million dollar media industry that it is.

Back in the day, only big companies could afford to advertise on TV, and only wealthy
media companies could afford to produce TV shows and news broadcasts that tapped into advertisers
pockets.

Today, you are as equally powerful as Fox News or AMC.

You have access to the largest broadcasting network in the world; Youtube.

You even share the same Advertiser market that Fox News or AMC does; Apple, Ford, General Mills etc.

The difference is that you don't have the large subscriber base that your competitors do.

If that scares you, let me remind you that this book hinges on sensational media, specifically spinning
the news.

If Fox News can capitalize on a sensational story, so can you. In fact you have a bit more liberty to get
creative with your stories than a traditional news syndicate does because they have to be conservative (I
mean that in the context of whatever subscriber base you cater to.)

The New York Times, Salon and Drudge Report are all good examples of "spinning the news" to fit a
certain demographic.

These media corporations are also the most successful. Because they direct the spin to whatever
demographic they've tailored their business plan to.

Salon writes articles for progressives and Drudge writes articles for Conservatives.

Before we're too lost in the woods, Johnny B Truant is just repeating what I have said all along;

"Your machines won't work without the right processor" or "Adsense won't work without an
exceptional business plan."

Chapter 7
Service and Maintenance

Though many content creators reading this will disagree, getting banned is not the end of the world. I have heard kids bewailing their fate because their one and only channel was suspended and their money was cut off.

I hope that's not you. You are the smart, clean cut, business minded individual that respects this financial institution for what it is.

Sometimes even the best of us make mistakes, and it's not the end of the world.

#1   You should understand this is a financially regulated business

#2   A suspension is only 3 MONTHS! it used to be 6 MONTHS and I believe over time as Youtube simplifies it's regulatory practices this system will be more streamlined.

You shouldn't be betting on Youtube creating shorter suspension times though, you should be focusing on not triggering violations that get you banned.

The rules are very simple, but you MUST follow them to the letter. RELAX. You are a media mogul. This is your business, I am going to teach you how to win, and this is nothing to get upset about.

Let's break this down Barney style, because I know some of you might skip this chapter and only come back to it after you're channel's been terminated. The first core principle is actually pretty simple; respect.

In Youtube's own words:

"We're not asking for the kind of respect reserved for nuns, the elderly, and brain surgeons. Just don't abuse the site. Every cool, new community feature on YouTube involves a certain level of trust. We trust you to be responsible, and millions of users respect that trust. Please be one of them."

Don't look for loopholes.

This means, if you have to go research videos to see if your strategy or content is going to get you banned...

it probably means you're going to get banned.

Asking the question; "Hey I have a song I'd like to use but I don't have the content license for it, but it's on a free song website" is kind of like saying; "hey I didn't read the rules about citing my content license for the song, do you think anyone will notice?"

Obviously if you didn't cite the content license you've already broken a rule.

How long it takes before someone flags your video is debatable and if you want to gamble your money for 3 months while Youtube makes a decision be my guest.

There is a good reason music is at the top of my list of things to get suspended for, naturally because it's the number one strike people get against them.

Having music for your videos is pretty important, but it's not impossible or as painstakingly difficult as you might think to find free or legit tunes.

Here is the most simple advice I can give you on music:

Only use Public Domain Music.

Even Classical Music recorded by let's say the London Symphony may have copyrights on the recording itself. So by searching for and downloading music with PUBLIC DOMAIN rights use, you will be protecting yourself from all angles.

All I had to do was type in: "Royalty Free Public Domain Music" into Google and there are thousands of options at my finger tips.

Next I simply cut and paste the link or description, providing a citation for my use of said music and I am done. It took me less than 10 seconds to do that.

Let's repeat this again; Public Doman music. Got it? See? Too easy.

Very quickly, let's just give the Microphone back to Youtube and let them explain in words an eighth grader could understand, how to keep from getting suspended:

Sex and Nudity

"YouTube is not for pornography or sexually explicit content. If this describes your video, even if it's a video of yourself, don't post it on YouTube." [And don't post Child Pornography, DUH!]

Harmful or Dangerous Crap

"Don't post videos that encourage others to do things that might cause them to get badly hurt, especially kids.

Videos showing such harmful or dangerous acts may get age-restricted or removed depending on their severity." I know what you're thinking; isn't this what makes UFC and MMA so popular? Yes. But as a civilized society we try to make these sports as honorable as possible. Just as Mike Tyson and Floyd Mayweather have been fined for being "un-honorable" we have to, in the same sense be cognizant of what makes dangerous sports or events "civilized" or "uncivilized."

Blood and Gore

"It's not okay to post violent or gory content that's primarily intended to be shocking, sensational, or disrespectful. If posting graphic content in a news or documentary context, please be mindful to provide enough information to help people understand what's going on in the video. Don't encourage others to commit specific acts of violence." [don't post a video of someone chopping a chicken head off without warning the audience Ms. Penny is about to be decapitated]

Also, if you noticed Youtube used my favorite word: "Sensational"

As a Content Creator/Media Mogul this is the word you LIVE and BREATHE by. Youtube just has rules about which topics they prefer you sensationalize.

Hateful Content

There seems to be a fine line here, ask Milo Yiannopoulos the Gay Conservative that got banned from Twitter for inciting a racially charged Twitterstorm against actress Leslie Jones. Let me be as blunt as I possibly can on this subject, using your channel to create hype and controversy is the fastest way to be a successful media mogul. But you must tread lightly and be conscious and aware of the commentary and dialogue that ensues. Be prepared to nip bad behavior in the bud. Political News for me is my biggest money making machine- but it also regularly attracts a viral overload of angry trolls.

With that said, anything else outside of accidentally triggering a race war is common sense.

Don't hate, don't post hateful videos. Don't discriminate for any reason (DUH!)

Spam, misleading metadata, and scams "Everyone hates spam. Don't create misleading descriptions, tags, titles, or thumbnails in order to increase views. It's not okay to post large amounts of untargeted, unwanted or repetitive content, including comments and private messages"

This is pretty easy kids, don't make a video to scam your viewers and don't spam the universe with links to your channels.

Don't make a video of a kitten and label the title; "Watch as Kitten gets Killed"

Sure, you may get a million views, but you'll have more angry PETA people flagging your video for abusive Title-Baiting than it's worth. Just don't do it.

Threats

Obviously, use your brain, don't ever use any of your channels to threaten someone or engage in stalking behavior (DUH!)

Copyright

This is the most important part of all the community guidelines and the main reason you're monetization could get suspended or your channel terminated.

"Respect copyright. Only upload videos that you made or that you're authorized to use. This means don't upload videos you didn't make, or use content in your videos that someone else owns the copyright to, such as music tracks, snippets of copyrighted programs, or videos made by other users, without necessary authorizations."

Caveat:

"In its most general sense, a fair use is any copying of copyrighted material done for a limited and "transformative" purpose, such as to comment upon, criticize, or parody a copyrighted work. Such uses can be done without permission from the copyright owner." -Rich Stim I HIGHLY RECCOMEND you read RIch Stim's book; Getting Permission: How to License & Clear Copyrighted Materials Online and Off 2013. You can buy the book used off Amazon for less than ten bucks. As a content creator, this needs to be on your shelf!

Tell me again, why I should buy that book?

Posting the legal description of the Fair Use Act on your video and understanding how it works, enables you to use any kind of media in your videos as long as it adheres to the rules.

That is how highly successful video channels like Young Turks or TMZ can scalp videos from The Associated Press or other Paparazzi sources and use them- as long as they follow the rules and guidelines laid out in the Fair Use Act.

Unfortunately I cannot compile everything you need to know about copyrighted material in this book, because it would be a text book, but I can give you some resources to help you stay out of trouble.

Meg Kribble of the Harvard Law School Library compiled an extensive list of places to find free content: Finding Public Domain & Creative Commons Media.

It is an especially smart place for novices to get their feet wet by using content that is 100% public domain. On the list are countless websites to find video, music and pictures. Let me repeat: Novices.

You must eventually learn to use copyrighted content in a way that is both legal and fair. The only way to do this is to study the book I mentioned above and also read:
Clearance & Copyright: Everything You Need to Know for Film and Television by Michael T. Donaldson.
Buy both Rich Stim and Michael Donaldson's books and put them under your pillow at night if you have to! Read and re-read them.

This is the only way you can be confident you are making the right choices when using copyrighted material.

Help! I've been Suspended!

Either you didn't read the two books I mentioned or you didn't follow the community guidelines. Trust me, Youtube is not on a witch hunt.
The sucky thing about getting suspended is that Adsense will stop across all the channel accounts. It's guilty by association.
I feel your pain. Though I have been in your shoes before, it has been years since any of my accounts were suspended. Reading this book is like benefiting from all the trials and tribulations I went through. The goal is to get your content buttoned up to the point you will never have to worry about getting suspended again.

First of all, as I mention below- don't delete the video that got you suspended, I explain that further on. Second, don't stop creating content. Your Adsense account will be turned on once Youtube reviews the case. It could take as long as 3 months, but do not count on it taking that long, go about your business as if it didn't happen. After you have disputed the suspension and fixed the issue, you will begin making money again. Even if it takes three months to get going, think about how many videos that is across ten channels. A lot. If you make just one video per week, that's 40 videos a month, which is 120 videos in three months. You cannot afford to take that kind of a loss.

When your Monetization kicks in, the compounding interest from all ten channels with 120 videos will more than make up for the time lost.
Though suspension seems like a thoroughly nasty part of life as a Media Mogul, I can assure you these types of bumps in the road happen in every sector of business.
Real Estate investors run into code violations all the time when buying and flipping property. One code violation can lead to expensive permits that may take months to get approved by the city. No work can be done until the proper permits are in place. Each day that passes with no progress ends up costing the Real Estate developer hundreds of thousands of dollars.
There are hiccups in any sector regulated by money, it's part of life- just get used to it.
On the positive side, as a content creator these channels cost you no money to keep in place. You may have an interruption in money generation but you are not losing money. Change how you look at money in this business, think like Newton.

What do I do if one of my videos has a strike against it?

Do NOT I repeat ; *do not* delete any videos that have any of the following issues:

Terms of Service strike
Copyright strike
Third-party global block claim
Terms of Use strike
Community Guidelines strike
Deleting videos containing these problems will make it impossible to fix the issues on your channel and therefore impossible to restore your channel to good standing.
If the strike against your channel is legitimate, don't file a dispute through YouTube until you've obtained a license for use of the content in question.

When you should delete comments to prevent de-Monetization.
You will not have time to monitor every comment made in your videos, but there is one simple step we need to take to ensure you don't have to.
Now don't get me wrong, you need to let people argue and discuss in the comments- it helps your keywords. But if they're cursing a lot, that negatively effects the quality of the video. Believe it or not, if there's too much cursing in the video comments you'll ultimately lose the ability to monetize your videos.

Go to your Creator Studio click "Community"
Then go down to "Community Settings"
From there, you're going to find the section where it says "Blacklist"
Here is where you want to put the raunchiest, foul, dirty words you can think of. Essentially, you want to put any and all words here that you want Youtube to block.
This prevents crawlers from downgrading your cost per click due to vulgar language (or potentially eliminate monetization altogether.)
Another essential problem you need to be able to recognize is COMPETITOR TROLLS.
These are other content creators with similar channels that only come to your channel to spam the comment section with abusive comments they know will get your channel deleted. They may or may not use cuss words, but cyber-bullying is a technicality that Youtube may suspend your account over so the best approach to this is vigilance. Though competitor trolls are generally ignored by other people, if you spot a comment thread getting out of hand, delete it as soon as possible.
This maintenance on your channel is part of the "Routine Maintenance" I talk about in this book.
Eventually you will be able to hire a content manager to do tasks like this, but for now- and with 2-10 channels it is a rudimentary task you must stay on top of.

How to further prevent your channels from getting banned or terminated

By now you are aware of all the major infractions that can result in having your channels de-monetized or terminated. Copyright infringement, using other people's videos, music in the background etc., etc. But here are a couple ways that an honest mistake can hurt you big:

Anytime you are producing a video related to a product, place, service etc, always understand that companies routinely have their Public Relations (PR) people scanning the web for negative videos that could affect sales.

They can't stop you from making a negative video, but they can report you if they feel your video is misleading or contains errors that have a bad impact on their product etc.

For instance, your video may be about the New F350 Diesel truck, and if you place a thumbnail on your video with a half-naked model riding in the back of an older model, a Ford employee may use that against you. They can flag your video under the guise that the model is not in the video (which Youtube labels as misleading) or even flag the video because the truck is an older model.

From my experience, this is typical of big corporation PR that just try to find any way to bully content creators that make a video of their product they don't like.

So be wary of that, because as a general rule, most run of the mill viewers do not report such trivial grievances with your videos. If your video is about kittens playing with a ball of string it's not likely that a viewer will flag your video for having a Playboy Bunny holding a kitten. On a rare occasion a prudish viewer may flag provocative thumbnails, but by and large Youtube will not ban a channel for just anyone. If Ford Corporation files a complaint or flags your video, it is almost a sure thing that Youtube would rather ban a small channel than face extensive legal fees filed by a big corporation.

Chapter 8
Hiring Workers

If you learn anything from this chapter, it is my hope that you understand how important the creative juices in your brain are.

If you have never read Timothy Ferris' book; "The 4-Hour Workweek: Escape 9-5, Live Anywhere, and Join the New Rich" then I highly encourage you to do so.

In his book, Tim talks about how important it is to free up time in your busy life to come up with new ideas and strategies for getting rich.

I'm going to ride his coat tails on this and suggest you apply his strategies to balancing your daily/weekly/monthly workloads with plenty of relaxing/vacation time.

We are most creative and innovative when we are not stressed and not consumed with making money. It may not seem like you are making money by outsourcing 10 videos per week to other people, but if you have followed this strategy from the beginning, you will know that even if each gig you order costs $5, and you make ten videos;
$50 is not going to affect your bottom line. Initially it may be half of your operating costs, but as you expand your subscriber base, it will pay for itself and you'll see the immediate return on investment. Your videos will be compounding interest, and in double the time (90 days after monetization) you are leveraging the viewership of 240 videos. That's a lot of money, no matter how you cut the pie.

The most valuable asset in your company is YOU. YOUR ideas, YOUR time and YOUR energy.

Just trust me on this, and give yourself the needed break.

When I had successfully established ten channels with 10 videos per week, I was exhausted. I was working full time, and bringing in barely enough to keep my utilities turned on.

The money I paid to freelancers who helped me create my videos was often the only money I had left for entertainment or eating out.

I ate a lot of Ramen and watched a lot of Netflix in those days! My point is, that I wasn't rich and certainly didn't have the money that most people believe a media manager needs to outsource their work.

As I mentioned in earlier chapters, be careful about what work you outsource.
Don't outsource people to create the scripts or write the stories. That's YOUR job.
YOU need to create the momentum and capitalize on the sensationalism of trending news stories.

The only things you should be outsourcing are video editing, voice overs/acting and creative design (for logos, intros/outros etc.)

Without further Ado- let me introduce you to the websites that I personally use for my businesses.
I selected these based on the price and quality of work.
I can pay with a credit or debit card, and the transaction is quick and easy.
Work is delivered on time and I am always satisfied with the results.

These are my top 7 places to find help at ridiculously low prices:

1. Fiver

Fiver wins as my absolute, hands down best choice for hiring other people to do your content editing. I like Fiver because I can come here for voice overs, actors, video creators and script writers- all in one place. The name "Fiver" comes from the Five Dollar price of most projects. I have paid as much as $40 for one service, but that was rare, and it required heavy technical editing not related to Youtube. As a general rule I pay about $5 for someone to read a script or read the script in front of a camera.

2. Upwork

Upwork wins as the freelance giant of the outsourcing industry and is the largest network by a long shot. The result of a merger between two large freelance job sites, oDesk and Elance, Upwork currently has 9 million workers in its network and 1.5 million clients. The service overs a wide range of freelance jobs that can be done remotely, including content designers, video software editors and script writers. Upwork offers hourly and fixed price proposals that be updated as you go along. A review rating scheme allows you to look through worker profiles and choose the best for your business.

3. 99Designs

99Designs is exclusively for designers, but it can be extremely helpful for projects that need new life breathed into them. I don't normally use this site because it uses a "crowdsource" type of putting a project online and waiting for people to bid on the project. Other people may find this useful, but working in media with time sensitive stories it proved to slow for my needs.

4. Guru

Started in 2001, Guru has completed 1 million jobs and received $200 million in payout. Today, Guru has 1.5 million freelancers on its website. In order to simplify the hiring search in such a large number of freelancers, employers can look through freelancer portfolios that include previous earnings and client reviews as well as skills and relevant experience. Freelancers in turn can get an idea of how reliable an employer is by looking at how much they have spent on freelancers in the past.

5. Crowded

Described as a "marketplace for on-demand workers," Crowded meets supply and demand problem with freelance job opportunities posted by clients. This website pulls freelance job postings from several on-demand platforms and makes them available to its network of virtual employees. The company was just founded in 2015, and already has 11,000 freelancers and 400 platform partners.

6. Freelancer

Freelancer boasts 17 million registered users, which is saying a lot. Many talented writers use this site, but I have not had the best success in hiring actors or script readers.

7. Toptotal

I put this at the very end because I have found the freelancers on here to be picky and most require higher pay for smaller projects. As a small fish just starting out, you may not find this suitable for your needs. Later on, if you decide to grow your business this would be a great place to find a content creator or assistant.

So here's another tip from someone that has been using freelancers for seven years- you will only need these sites to prospect for new creatives initially.

Eventually you will find the people you like and only go to them when you need something. You'll learn to trust them and they will learn what your personal style is. It makes your life a lot easier down the road! Just starting up is going to mean you have to meet new friends and probably trust people more than you normally would. Most of my best creative friends are from places like India and the United Arab Emirates. That isn't to say I never use American or European creatives because I do-- especially voice overs and actors. But if I need video editing, splicing, uploading- any kind of technical help, I usually delegate this overseas.

These are the smiling faces that will help you turn your business into a wealthy enterprise, so treat them with respect and reward them for their hard work!

Chapter 9
You're Rich Now Be Careful

When your stats have kicked your 90 day portfolio until full gear, you will truly begin to see the magic behind how quickly pennies, dimes and quarters add up.

The mistake I made when outsourcing content creation to freelancers, was delegating the wrong tasks.

It's easy to fall into the greed trap when you see the dollars and cents adding up every day.

There is a special kind of mystical or magical connection with the creation of good content. You can hire people to make videos, to read your scripts and even get in front of the cameras for you- but the story... the actual story itself... must be yours.

It must come from your mind and be a product of your own unique vision. The moment you stop creating is the moment this system doesn't work.

You may think I'm exaggerating, but it's true; if you hire someone to be the vision behind the stories you create, you are essentially working yourself out of a job.

This is why YOU as a small fish have the advantage over "Big fish." Big media dogs have to hire expensive recruiting and sourcing teams to find creative geniuses. Even then, they are not guaranteed to get more than a snotty nosed kid fresh out of school or worse, an out of touch clanker that knows nothing about SEO.

If you're reading this book, you are an entrepreneur! Even better, you're a creative entrepreneur!

You are not just knocking doors asking for a job, you are reading this book to create a job!

I have been in recruiting, sourcing and creative management for a long time, and I can tell you that people like you and me are hard to find.

At some point you will have to make the decision to either stay in creative production or move on to media project management. As a small fish you are both creative producer and project manager. If you want to simply be a creative producer you can, for as long as you like. But the moment you hang up your creative producer hat, you better have a game plan. Your game plan better include a clone of yourself that will take your hat and wear it just as well as you did. Your business relies on it.

The tricky part of hiring a good content producer is that they can walk out on you at any time. In which case you will need to either have a backup apprentice content producer (i.e.; assistant content producer) or be ready to take the reins and wear both hats.

The content producer is the life blood of a media business, treat it as such.

You may be curious as to what a media project manager does, and it's pretty simple; you are already doing it by outsourcing to workers that create the videos, do the voiceovers or act in front of the camera.
The difference is, you will relinquish the management of those creative professionals to a content manager. Your only job will be seeking out new talent or new niche markets to capitalize on.

Whether it's finding Youtubers that have dynamic personalities and offering them contracts or buying people out of their channels for ownership rights- you are essentially looking for new channels to add to your portfolio.

When you have identified a new channel or niche that you want to develop, you will pull together a new team of creative individuals to manage that channel.

In the next five years it is my prediction that Youtube will become more and more regulated. I believe contract negotiations will get more complex and Youtube production studios will rival TV production studios.

This is already happening in many applications, but most people don't see it evolving.

If you are a college student reading this book, my advice is to quit whatever degree program you are in and focus exclusively on broadcast journalism and video editing.
I have looked at many online and conventional universities and colleges and they are still behind the curve.
There are plenty of separate degree programs out there that teach traditional journalism and traditional video editing, but nothing (yet) that focuses primarily on Youtube production and Adsense Monetization.

I promise you that soon, maybe within this next decade, there will actually be college level classes built entirely on virtual commerce, specifically Adsense and Adwords.

So if you want to make a lot of money, and you're on the fence about what to do with your life, an investment in these types of courses will take you a long, long way.

Maybe you think you're too old to jump on the band wagon, but it is not too late for anyone to take advantage of this emerging job market.

SEO certification and web optimization classes can help you get an edge on Production Management.

Think big! Think like a big fish and follow the money.

This is actually the "last" chapter of the book (The Tool Bag is a DIY reference bonus.)

I want to use this last portion to give you some pointers on "staying financially fit" as a new millionaire or six-figure earnings winner.

I know I'm going to get a lot of backlash for telling people to "outsource their work" to other countries. I guess I just think differently than other people, because the money I make I end up spending on innovation and building business that improves the American economy that I live in.

So it's probably going to make people upset that I recommend "workcations" in other countries like Thailand or Peru, where the cost of living is dramatically lower.

Most metro areas in these places cater to Expats and wealthy business gurus. Lima Peru actually has a Starbucks with most modern amenities (including high speed internet) to lure budget conscious entrepreneurs to their country.

Most roundtrip tickets to South America can be found for less than a grand. If you are looking to get away for a month and cut your living expenses in half, look into the top 10 cheapest places to vacation.

Luxury room and board for under $500 a month? Yes please!

So think of it this way; if you're airplane ticket costs $1,000 and Room+Board for $500 a month you could literally get away with a $1,500 vacation and work from your latop at a fraction of the US or UK cost.

Here is the next thing you need to have on your travel itinerary; Youtube Events and Conferences! VidCon, VidSummet, Beautycon, Itatube (just to name a few) are growing EVERY year.

These are the people you need to be rubbing shoulders with and meeting network owners that could eventually become partners.

If money is an issue, pack a bag and make a road trip out of it, the conferences are totally worth it.

Building on other people's momentum and creative juices will amplify yours!

Some of the conferences are tailored to specific creators like "make-up and style divas" or "alternative news journalists" so do your research and keep note of the events that best fit your personal strategy.

Building a 120 video, 10 channel portfolio in 90 days is the fastest way to hit six figures.

Learn to follow news related to Youtube! Add Youtube's official Spotlight channel to your daily vitamin mix:
youtube.com/user/YouTube

Learn to identify how Youtube rewards the innovators it spotlights and ape them.

Subscribe to Google's Youtube page: youtube.com/user/Google

This is the channel Google employees watch to stay current on trends within the company! Start looking at yourself as a "Google partner" or "outsourced employee" instead of a lowly "video maker."

Make the dynamics of Youtube's creative community work for you!

Get your Google + Profile connected with ANY content creators you can find! Put Youtubers in your circles and watch SEOMoz videos with Rand Fishkin to see how linking your circles creates more traffic!

shhhhhh (I shouldn't be giving you all the secrets!)

But listen people, Youtube wants you to be smarter. It wants to help you free up your time to be inspired and create good content! There is soooooo much money to be made, you just need to broaden your perspective on this game to make it work to your advantage.

This short and sweet $3 investment is not meant to be the know-all be-all of Youtube (trust me, even the executives at Youtube are scrambling for the gold, and it keeps getting better every year!)

To make a textbook would miss the intended audience and dilute the key principles of success. What I have created for you is the roadmap to get you into the financial bracket you want to be in. Take everything you've learned here and apply it with tenacity and diligence and you WILL be rewarded.

Good luck on your adventure and have don't forget to have fun in the process!

Chapter 10
The Tool Bag

I realize that most of my readers are probably skilled Youtubers. But I wanted to ensure that even novices could utilize this chapter and save a little money from having to purchase "How-To Guides."

These topics are here because they must be a part of the creator's repertoire. You must master these and know them in and out, from top to bottom.

Also, I wanted to include some other books that have changed my life and may do the same for you. I realize many people have already read them, but I've found most video-creatives do not usually stray into the marketing and business section.

These books are:

1. Guerilla Marketing by Jay Conrad Levinson
2. Truth, Lies & Advertising: The Art of Account Planning by Jon Steel
3. Drive by Daniel Pink
4. Rules for Revolutionaries by Guy Kawasaki
5. Fascinate by Sally Hogshead
6. Trust Me I'm Lying by Ryan Holiday
7. The Brass Check by Upton Sinclair
8. Think and Grow Rich by Napolean Hill
9. Who Moved my Cheese? by Spencer Johnson
10. Rich Dad Poor Dad by Robert Kiyosaki and Sharon Lechter

For the ambitious that do not read this chapter, the only thing I ask is that you read over ther Copyright Laws and Fair Use Act to gain a clear understanding of the definitions and verbiage needed to use other people's content.

In this chapter we cover:

1. How to set up an Adsense Account; Tax ID and Account PIN.

2. How to turn on Monetization for your videos

3. Copyright Laws and Fair Use Act

4. Video editing, Screen Capture and Uploading Basics

How to set up an Adsense Account; Tax ID and Account PIN.

As you know, AdSense has updated the account approval process to include the following steps:

Sign up for AdSense
Monetize your videos
Wait while your account is reviewed and either accepted or rejected (this is the part where an actual human takes a look at the quality of your channel and attaches a virtual credit score to your channel)

Step-by-Step Guide to Creating an AdSense Account:

First, go to the Signup page for AdSense.

You will see an option to create a new Google account,(as suggested, I reccomend you create a new Gmail account if you are trying the 90 day, 10 channel strategy) or you can choose to use your existing Google account.

Create AdSense Gmail account (follow prompts on website, refer to the IMPORTANT steps on creating multiple channels found in "Building the Machines/Chapter 3")

Create AdSense account

This form is straight-forward. You simply need to enter your website address and select the content language. For the website URL use your Channel address.

AdSense contact information:

This is the most important part.

The "payee name" is very important. Make sure to use the same name under which you have a bank account, as AdSense will be sending you checks or EFT payment under that name.

If you make a mistake here, changing the payee name of your account will be difficult.

There is a long list of countries which are not allowed to change the payee name after signing up, so ensure your bank account name and payee name are exactly the same.

Next add your contact information and fill in the other details.

Accept AdSense policies.

Read the AdSense policies and put a checkmark in all three boxes.

Once done, click on "Submit", and on the next page you can review your details.

Make sure that all the details are accurate and up to date!

Signing up with your email account:

(Must read: Google AdSense new account approval process)

Submit Adsense Tax Information

Once you have signed up for AdSense,the AdSense team will review your application again after you've added the channels and turned on Monetization for your videos. Your account will be activated with an Adsense Pin that will be sent to you.

All of this can take up to 1-2 months depending upon your geographical location (it is only a few days for US residents with no mistakes in the application)

Once everything is set up, in order to get paid from AdSense you need to complete two further steps:

Submit your tax information
Enter your pin
You will need to submit a tax form specific to how you are conducting business.

AdSense Pin:

You will receive an AdSense Pin by mail once you reach the threshold of $10. You need to add the pin to your AdSense account.

You will start receiving payment once your AdSense account reaches the $100 threshold.

How to turn on Monetization for your videos

To begin, log-in to your YouTube channel account.
In the Channel Settings tab, select "Enable monetization."

Follow the steps to accept the YouTube monetization agreement.

In the Uploads tab, you will see a green box with a dollar sign next to the videos that are immediately eligible for monetization.

Videos that are not eligible to be monetized due to copyright will be appear under the Copyright Notices tab.
(Again, it is crucial all of your videos have the correct citations and labels that link viewers to the original content and/or include the copyright ownership details attributing the work to the proper collaborators. Also ensure you place the copyright and fair use statement in description window of your videos)

Next, you'll need to associate an AdSense account to your YouTube channel.

It is free to set up a new AdSense account. (See the above steps in Setting up an Adsense account)

You will need either a PayPal or a bank account and a valid mailing address in order to have your account verified.

AdSense will update you by mail once your account has been approved.

You can also associate an existing, approved AdSense account to your channel (be advised, I do not recommend linking your personal accounts with business accounts for ANY reason)
Use this option only for chain-linking all 10 of the channels you have created in Chapter 3 to Adsense account.

Copyright Laws and Fair Use

Now don't get me wrong, there are many things I'd rather do than study fair use and copyright laws; such as stabbing myself in the eye with a fork or tumbling down a flight of stairs littered with thumb tacks.

But I, like you, had to learn the laws in order to run a successful business.

If you do not read the sections on fair use and how to properly vet the usage of other people's intellectual
property, you will probably end up at some point getting suspended or worse, banned. Even if that never

happens, it's likely you'll constantly be chasing videos that are getting de-monetized for failure to meet the code descriptions.

I have prepared these in a grade school level explanation. Don't be insulted if you feel like a two year old being coached on how to use a potty chair.

I just want to make sure you clearly understand it so you never have to go through the excruciating pain of reading the technical parts of copyright laws and fair use again.

Copyright:

A thing is invented, and its design and other things are involved. There are chances that others can also copy the same thing. To stop this from happening, copyright is the best option ("the definition of copyright",
2016).

Copyright is the law that gives the person the ownership over the things made by him or her.

Consider that I have made a video, photograph or any other thing.
If the work gets a copyright, then no one else can copy it or use it in the future.
It assures the ownership of the product.

There are many songs in a movie, but no one can copy it in the other.
This is all because of the copyright laws. These laws have protected the laws of the ones who have spent time on making something and have the risk to get copied, etc.

There are various copyright laws implemented. The rights they include are as follows:

- The right to reproduce work.
- To prepare the derivative works.
- To distribute copies
- To perform the work.
- To display the work properly.

Like this, there are many rights which are protected by the copyright laws and need to be checked on.

Thus, the thing is that if a product is made, that work cannot be used by the other without the consent of the one who bears the copyright on the work.

Such things matter a lot and are necessary for protecting the person's rights and privacy.

From this, the main goals of copyright are to encourage the development of the culture, science, and innovation, nonetheless providing the financial benefit to the copyright holders for their work and facilitate their access to knowledge and entertainment for the public.

We can recognize it as intellectual property, having trademarks, and rights of publicity ("1. What is a Copyright? - Plagiarism Today", 2016).

Copyright Duration:
The duration of copyright varies from country to country. It all depends on the type of work.
Like the minimum period of copyright in a literary work is equal to the life of the author plus the fifty years. This varies from country to country too ("About Copyright - Copyright Clearance Center", 2016).

Implied Licenses:
An implied copyright license created by the law, generally in the absence of an actual agreement between the parties. These arise when the conduct of the parties signifies the license to be extended between the copyright owner and the licensee. At the same, the parties don't need to create the license.

Not only this, it allows the licensee to use the copyrighted work and is necessary too.

Thus, this license grants the licenses in various situations where the copyrighted works created by the one party on request of another.
Overall, all such factors matter a lot and should be considered performing various works including stuff that is copyrighted by the owner.

The one who needs to use the copyrighted matter needs to be aware of the various Copyright and the Fair Use laws that need to be kept in mind using the copyrighted content.

These are explained below:

This is explained as the courts tried to balance the rights of the copyright owners with society's use and allowing them copying and usage of the matter in a judicious way (i.e.; journalism and broadcast media)

At the same, fundamental belief that all copying shouldn't be restricted, but the level should be reduced to some extent.

Take for instance use of the word; "Googling" in the context of "searching online for a word."
Google is a trademarked word, so in the sense every time someone wished to use this word, they would need to request permission first. This system would be lengthy and expensive.

The factors considered under the fair use act are as follows:

There is a need to recognize the purpose for which it's being used, ie; for commercial use or any educational purpose. This needs to be specified and is necessary.

The nature of the copyrighted work.

The amount and the substantiality of the portion used the copyrighted work as a whole.

Also considering the effect of the extent of the copyrighted work ("Fair Use in Copyright (BitLaw)", 2016).

Need for video content creators to use copyrighted materials:

There is a need for the one who makes online videos to interpret the copyright doctrine of fair use.

The thing is that video is becoming the central part of everyday communication.

People are even using it on the digital platform. People make and share videos to tell the stories about their personal lives, remixing of popular songs and videos etc.

In this arena, video mixing has become the component of political discourse. There are times when people simply mixed various songs and videos and experienced various copyright issues. So, there is an emerging need to understand the process of this copyright system.

It is to be realized that more and more creation and sharing of videos depends upon the ability to use and circulate the existing copyrighted work.

This fact is not recognized whereas it is amongst the most important.
There are times when such digital videos are not promoted at a bigger level, but on the digital platform things are becoming more developed and leading to the development of new business.

At the same time, the legal status of inserting the copyrighted work into new work will also become important and necessary.

Thus, it is important for the video makers, online service providers, and content providers to understand the legal rights of the makers of the new culture.

Then only various things will be done in a lawful manner (with as much integrity and respect as possible.)

Mashups and remixes are among the latest online trends. They are changing the traditional culture with the upcoming new trend. The cultural value of copying is so important and is well established in the hearts of the copyright law. There is a need to give limited rights to the creators and provide them the time, culture and the chance to use the copyright material without the permission. But this may even hurt the sentiments and lead to several issues too.

The video makers thus, can gain help from the various groups working on fair use. We can understand it by a simple example of how historians keep records of their writings and updated them after particular intervals of time.

The same happens in the commercial media. The fair use is very important in the daily news being broadcasted and classical television programs and much more.

Thus, there is a need to determine such factors and the conditions in which they occur and what all can be done in the aspect of getting the copyright.

At the same time, it doesn't work against the fair laws made for the betterment of others.
Though traditional videos are made, there are many non-professional and personal video makers who often create their videos. These videos are generally outside the marketplace and share a delimited network, thus, enjoying copyright advantages.
Also, they are more likely to receive the special considerations under the fair use doctrine.

The key point should be to never forget the main motive of the fair use doctrine and following the criteria as specified in it.

These principles squarely root the concept of transformativeness. This transformativeness describes the person's time and creative energy utilized in producing the mashup, a personal video or some other work.

At the same time, the new things being included should be recognized, and properly supported to to elevate the copyrighted product to the status of the new product.

Always credit the original creator of content used and always cite your sources with links if possible.

Principle and limitation of the copyrighted material:
Principle: Video makers need the best, unique work for project utilization. Comment and the critique are at the core of fair use doctrine, to safeguard the freedom of expression. The various comments and quotes are there which even describe the basic quality of the work. It needs to be realized that the critique plays an important role in determining the quality of the quoted work. The work should be done in a proper manner and should not hurt the sentiments of other people.

In the most basic sense, any video you make that comments on a video made by someone else (ie; ABC NEWS) can comment on the story outlined in the video, but cannot critique the video quality or video product itself (i.e.; camera, company or media organization)

Limitation: The use should not be done in such a way that it abolishes from being a critique and just becomes a way to satisfy the audience's taste. Thus, it should not become a market substitute for getting the work.

Again, you should not make a channel that copies every single video segment of Jimmy Fallon's nightly show. If viewers came to your channel strictly to see Jimmy Fallon and not to listen to your critique, this would be a violation of the copyright law.

Using copyright material just to provide an example:
Principle: There are times when the copyrighted material is used by the video makers to give an example.
Writers, generally in print media use various quotations of words and images.
This being done by illustrating a video maker's critique of another video and doesn't affect the law of fair use.

At the same, it is fair if the video makers don't use the quoted material for making new things.
(I.e.; You cannot quote The President's speech in its entirety to incorporate it into a speech of your own." (I.e.; You cannot quote another Youtuber's opening line "Hey you beautiful bodacious Babies! It's me again!" and use this as your opening line- this would be creating new content with the copyrighted line every time you made a new video. You can however critique how "ridiculous" such an opening line would be in a new video, which would not be violating copyright law.

Limitations: The proper material being there is often likely to reduce the likelihood of the complaints or other legal actions against the fair use claim.

If you use content from another video, make sure you properly cite the video and provide a link to the creator's channel.

Using copyrighted material accidentally:
Principle: Video makers at times, record copyrighted sounds, and images. This occurs in everyday recordings.
This occurred when the filming was done, a copyrighted song was being played in the background and got recorded in the film also. In such cases, the makers need to remove the reality to some extent. The creative video makers can be helped by the fair use because the material they seek is in reality. Thus, making that the new creativity of the person won't be cheated by the other.

Youtube understands that we live in a real world with real events going on around us. Youtube understands that once a video has been recorded of real life activities, certain copyrighted logos, pictures, words and sounds may accidentally be included in the video.
To prevent unnecessary exposure to copyright violations, always place a notice on every video recorded in a public venue as such;

"Any unintended recording or accidental usage of any copyrighted content in the making of this video is not the sole intention of the creator. In accordance with the Fair Use Act, the content of this video is for educational and public communication only, with no ownership or rights to content of any kind implied or expressed."

Limitation: For taking advantage of the fair use act, it is necessary for the maker to determine that the music or any other copyrighted material wasn't used on demand and had been used accidentally because of said reasons.
Getting to this is quite difficult. Thus, it's better to be careful when all this is being performed ("Code of Best Practices in Fair Use for Online Video - Center for Media and Social Impact", 2016)

Not only this, various online video hosting sites like You Tube are providing the opportunity to the user generated content (UGC) on the internet. These services enabling are easily availed by the people and has led to the explosion of creativity by the people. Various people have actively taken part in this activity and have represented their creativity in a variety of ways.

Overall, we can consider this step being successful.
But at the same, there are times when the creators post things which are wrong and can easily affect the sentiments of the other people. This needs to be controlled. There are times when the students being indulged in educational trips capture or record things which are offensive. Sometimes, it may lead to violence too. This needs to be checked, controlled and worked on. For this, a verification cell should be there for authorizing the uploading of various videos ("Fair Use Principles for User Generated Video Content", 2007).

These factors need to be controlled and at the same, following tips can also be followed:
The sound is very important in making any video. Thus, in today's technology, various sorts of audio or easily available on the internet. Rather than using the original track, the music with combined with various sound effects can be used. If the person is unable to make his audio it is better to hire the person/expert in doing the same. By doing so, the work becomes unique and being free from various offenses and the person has license to use it ("9 Copyright Laws Every Video Producer Should Know", 2012).

From the above, we can conclude that copywriting is very important in day to day life. It has changed the life of many people and has even helped them in exploring the creative mind.
We should realize that it is very easy to see how moral rights are useful for fighting against plagiarism. In the same, the role played by copyrights is very important.

Video editing, Screen Capture and Uploading Basics

This element of content creation can get a little tricky, due to the fact that Youtube is very selective about what content it allows to be used in a monetized video.
I want to use this opportunity to point out that you are not limited to using Adsense as a means to monetize your videos. In fact, there are a long list of Adsense competitors
to choose from when monetizing. While Adsense will also wait to generate a payment to you at the $100 mark, these ads enable you to recieve payment at lower values
(if you so choose.) Here a few:

Alternatives
BuySellAds
Banner Ads
$20 (Paypal) $50 (Check) $500 (Wire Transfer)

Propeller Ads
PopUnder Ads Mobile Ads Banner Ads
$50 (Paypal) $100 (Payoneer) $500 (Wire Transfer)

Chitika
Targeted Text Mobile
$10 (Paypal) $50 (Check)

Skimlinks
Skimlink Links
$10 (Paypal)

But getting back to content creation, my go to screen capture software is Screen Castify. I really only use a microphone to record my script and Screen Castify does the rest.
It videos my desktop; either full screen or just the web browser. This enables me to click through different videos that are relevant to the news story I am looking for.
There are screen recorders out there, but I cannot attest to how well they work because I have been a long time user of Screen Castify.
When my video is complete, I will often ad my intro and outro (a conclusion statement) and remove any bloopers, dead air or places in the video that I think don't flow.
Here are a few of the best video editors to start with (that won't break the bank)

Windows Movie Maker
Virtualdub
Wax
Avidemux
Ffmpeg

Blender
Lightworks

In college there was no single software that I ever heard of students gravitating to. Each software editor has their own benefits and you really need to test each one out to
see how it works with your style and level of knowledge.

One of the other tricks that I like to use, is setting up Google Hangouts to record a conversation with Web gurus so that I can later take parts of those videos and monetize them.

Technical videos especially in relation to a certain topic (i.e. Youtube Monetization) attract HUGE traffic!

What's crazy is that the web gurus in the conversation don't always need to be super stars to get traffic. Having a solid title to your video like; "How Ron Smith turned his Youtube
channel into a cash machine:" will be enough to encourage others to watch the show.

I also suggest investing in a quality microphone that is optimized for quality voice overs. If you are only using screen capture software, your voice and the quality of the sound is
what will make people watch your videos in their entirety.

Many foreign content creators that cannot speak english use word documents and text documents in their screen recording process to to communicate with the viewer.
I have seen many of these DIY, How-To videos with no voice get thousands of views! Imagine how many more views you'd get by actually talking!

The Filmmaker's Handbook: A Comprehensive Guide for the Digital Age by Stephen Ascher is my top pick for books on video editing along with valuable insight into
how to create dynamic content.

It's my hope that you will take everything you have learned here and create a profitable income from it. Good luck with your new business venture and remember;
never stop creating!

List of References

1. What is a Copyright? - Plagiarism Today. (2016). Plagiarism Today. Retrieved 15 September 2016, from
https://www.plagiarismtoday.com/stopping-internet-plagiarism/your-copyrights-online/1-what-is-a-copyright/
9 Copyright Laws Every Video Producer Should Know. (2012). Videomaker.com. Retrieved 15 September 2016, from
https://www.videomaker.com/article/c15/15953-9-copyright-laws-every-video-producer-should-know
About Copyright - Copyright Clearance Center. (2016). Copyright Clearance Center. Retrieved 15 September 2016,
from http://www.copyright.com/learn/about-copyright/
Code of Best Practices in Fair Use for Online Video - Center for Media and Social Impact. (2016).Center for
Media and Social Impact. Retrieved 15 September 2016, from http://cmsimpact.org/code/code-best-practices-fair-
use-online-video/
Fair Use in Copyright (BitLaw). (2016). Bitlaw.com. Retrieved 15 September 2016, from
http://www.bitlaw.com/copyright/fair_use.html
Fair Use Principles for User Generated Video Content. (2007). Electronic Frontier Foundation. Retrieved 15
September 2016, from https://www.eff.org/pages/fair-use-principles-user-generated-video-content
the definition of copyright. (2016). Dictionary.com. Retrieved 15 September 2016, from
http://www.dictionary.com/browse/copyright